Clutter
RESCUE!

Clutter
RESCUE!

JUST MINUTES A DAY TO GET ORGANIZED—FOREVER!

~~Anderson County Library~~
Anderson, S.C.
PEN

HEARST BOOKS
New York

contents

Foreword

This book is for anyone who has spent 20 minutes looking for the remote, moved homework to put dinner on the table, searched high and low for that favorite sweater—only to find it crumpled under a stack of dirty clothes—or missed paying a bill on time because it was stuffed in a junk drawer. If that sounds even a little bit like you, you're not alone. Almost everyone has to deal with a disorganized home to one degree or another.

It doesn't mean you're messy or a bad person—it's just that life is more hectic than ever. As we become busier and busier, the clutter just seems to take over. What's the answer? Develop solutions that win the war against clutter and banish messes forever.

At *Good Housekeeping*, we've created a system to do just that. By dividing each room into manageable zones and devoting less than an hour a day, you can get your home completely organized—in less than a month. After you've made the clutter-beating changes that are right for your home and your family, you'll have to spend no more than a few minutes each day to keep clutter from creeping back in. We've even included a "Maintaining" section at the end of each chapter to help you.

This complete plan for organizing is simple, logical, and realistic. We give you strategies for attacking each zone, and advice on how to reorganize all key areas and eliminate clutter throughout your home. Even if you don't have the time or energy to organize a whole room at once, you can probably find time to get it done zone by zone. We've included a clock icon to give you an idea of how much time you need to set aside to complete each one so you can plan when to tackle a zone based on how much time you have. (There's nothing worse than getting halfway through reorganizing a closet only to find that you have to run to pick up the kids, get to work, or do an errand.)

Clutter Rescue is not about "straightening up." It's not about how to clean better or faster. It's about making real changes that will alter the way you use the space in your home so that you don't create clutter in the first place. The fixes can be as simple as hanging a hook for your keys so you never misplace them, or as complex as outfitting your drawers with organizers so that everyone in the house knows exactly where things belong.

Clutter Rescue will help you avoid frustration. The task of organizing each zone is broken down into manageable chunks, so you'll never feel overwhelmed. We've also included helpful tips and insights: You'll find regular boxes called "Dollar Smart" that will help you save money and get good value from anything you buy to help you organize. "Storage in Style" boxes provide simple and quick ways to make your home look great with new organizational aids. And keep your eye out for the "Inside Scoop" boxes—they give you ingenious, little-known facts and strategies that will save you time and effort, and help you to avoid frustration. And if you want to learn more about specific organizing products and other information from the Good Housekeeping Research Institute, visit the *Good Housekeeping* Web site at www.goodhousekeeping.com.

So go ahead: Turn the page and take your first steps toward making your home permanently clutter free.

—Rosemary Ellis
Editor-in-Chief
Good Housekeeping

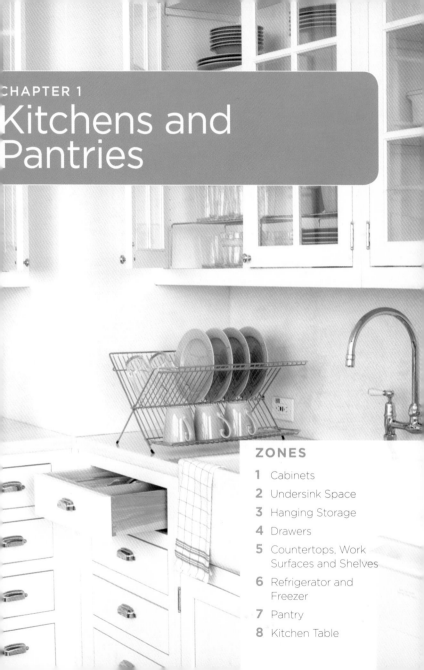

CHAPTER 1
Kitchens and Pantries

ZONES

Now more than ever, the kitchen is the center of the home. It's not unusual for the kids to do their homework at the kitchen table while one parent cooks and the other works on a laptop. With all the activity, it's no wonder the kitchen is typically the most cluttered room in the house.

Although organizing your kitchen may seem like a monumental task, the process for freeing it of clutter follows a basic principle. Simply put, every item in the kitchen should be stored near where it's going to be used, in a place that makes sense. This makes for an efficient work flow, which in turn makes for a much more pleasant work space, while ensuring that clutter is gone for good.

To help you organize each zone in the kitchen, you can choose from a large array of storage accessories found in stores. You just need to select the ones that are right for your kitchen and the way you use your space. You can also come up with your own homemade techniques, which may solve your challenges in less expensive, more innovative ways.

It's important to budget your time in the kitchen and not try to tackle the whole room at once. Trying to do more than one zone at a time can become overwhelming. Although the times listed for each zone are not going to vary much from person to person, you may not have all the zones in your home. For instance, you may not have an eat-in kitchen, so you won't have to bother with Zone 8 (Kitchen Table).

Just keep your eye on the goal: a permanently clutter-free kitchen.

OPPOSITE Shelves, cabinets, and drawers team up with spacious work surfaces to make this kitchen as functional as it is beautiful.

This stylish kitchen makes the most of a small space by using a variety of storage options where they make the most sense.

1

Glass-front cabinets add an attractive decorative element to the kitchen. Note the interior lights (center), which make finding plates and dishes easy— day or night.

2

Open shelving supports baskets that keep fresh fruits and vegetables in plain view and on hand for cooking—without using valuable counter space.

3

Undercounter drawers and cabinets, in a mix of different sizes, ensure that a variety of supplies and appliances can be efficiently stored. The drawers can also be outfitted with inserts, such as cutlery organizers and pan lid slots.

4

A customized pot rack was created by fitting the cooktop vent with rails to hang stainless-steel pans. The effect is as handsome as it is useful.

5

A hanging rail with utensils keeps kitchen tools right where the cook needs them—over the food-prep area.

ZONE 1
Cabinets ⏱ 1 HOUR

Begin with your cabinets. Working on one cabinet at a time, pull everything out and give the shelves a quick cleaning. Now assess what you've pulled out of the cabinet.

- Is it food, equipment, or supplies that will be used near where the cabinet is located? If not, these items should go somewhere else.
- Does the cabinet have a lot of extra room that is not being used efficiently? If so, the highest shelves might be best for rarely used items, such as special-occasion platters.
- Was everything crammed into the cabinet? If so, you'll need to find new places for some of what was there.

Take this opportunity to start shedding.

- Throw away open boxes of food staples that are more than 6 months old.
- Donate canned goods you've had for more than 9 months. You'll probably never use them if you haven't already. (Or include the cans in your emergency preparedness kit that you keep in a basement, garage, or large closet.)

DOLLAR SMART

Clearly Better: Why spend money on storage containers for loose dry goods when you can turn to your recycling bin for free, attractive containers? Clean, clear-glass wine bottles with tight-fitting corks intact make eye-catching containers for rice, sugar, ground coffee, and other fine-textured dry goods (use a funnel to fill them). The filled containers look great, and you'll find that pouring sugar out of a bottle is much easier than pouring it out of a bag.

A built-in column of slide-out wooden trays creates a handy in-kitchen pantry with plenty of storage space for food items large and small. Using trays or bins in a pantry helps keep odd-shaped containers in order.

- Discard or donate orphan glassware, dishes, or flatware whose mates have disappeared or been broken.
- Get rid of equipment and appliances you never use.

As you begin putting things back into the cupboard, group similar items together: cereals with grains, canned goods with other canned goods, and glassware with dishware. This will make finding everything much easier. Get in the habit of placing all food labels facing front and lining up glassware and dishes in neat rows and stacks. The goal is to make everything in your cabinets easy to see and reach, and to make it clear where things go when the dishwasher gets emptied or bags of groceries are being put away. There should be room around glasses and appliances so you can easily remove them without having to move other items out of the way.

Larger items, such as mixing bowls, waffle irons, and baking trays, generally go in undercounter cabinets. But if those cabinets are crowded, consider hanging pots, pans, and any other equipment with handles or loops (see Zone 3, page 23), or put them in the often-underused space above the cabinets.

Consider the following unique solutions for the different types of items you plan to store in your cabinets.

STORAGE IN STYLE

Out on a Ledge: One way to ensure that spices are where you need them, when you need them, is to use a spice ledge. This is a shallow shelf no more than 2 inches deep (you can buy premade ledges or make one yourself by staining [or painting] and hanging a length of 1-inch-by-2-inch board). Line up your spices along the ledge with labels facing out and they'll be right at hand and ready for use whenever you're cooking.

CANNED GOODS Make preparing meals easier by organizing canned goods by type (for example, fruit with fruit). The trick to keeping cans organized is maintaining visibility. There are a number of ways to ensure that you can clearly see which canned goods are where:

Tiered shelf platforms, available in wire or solid plastic, are ideal for keeping cans and jars in plain view. Many versions are available, including those that expand, slide out, and have hideaway trays.

Helper shelves are basic wire shelves with legs. They essentially double your cabinet shelf space because you can slide cans under the shelf and place others on top of it. Some types have adjustable legs for even more storage flexibility.

Turntables or lazy Susans keep groups of items in one easily accessible place within a cupboard. For example, place tomato sauce, paste, and canned diced tomatoes on a single shelf.

ABOVE LEFT Concealed behind a simple cabinet front, large slide-out trays organize pots and lids and contain plenty of room for small appliances, which are often bulky. ABOVE RIGHT Lazy Susan trays provide quick and easy access to pots and pans. They are especially useful in hard-to-reach areas, such as the recess in these corner cabinets.

SPICES Put spice jars in a tiered wire or wooden spice platform that lets you store them with the labels out. "Pull-down" versions can also make it easier to reach the spices. A spice carousel is another option. Sometimes making sure that spices are as close as possible to the cooking area means getting them out of the cabinet; see other spice storage options in Zones 3, 4, and 7 (pages 23, 26, and 39, respectively). Regardless of where you put them, spices should be kept out of direct light and away from heat sources.

ABOVE LEFT A handy, compact spice carousel fits neatly in this cabinet with plenty of room to turn to reveal the spices a cook may need. ABOVE RIGHT Use a tiered cabinet organizer to arrange bottled or canned goods to make the best use of cabinet space, and to make it easier to find what you need.

STORAGE IN STYLE

Check Your Bags: Get the plastic grocery bags that you use for garbage under control by stuffing them into a plastic milk jug, oversize soda bottle, or an empty laundry detergent bottle that you keep wherever you store cleaning supplies. Here's how: Clean the jug or bottle, cut a 2-inch hole in the side, and stuff the bags into the container. When you need a bag, just pull one out. As an alternative, keep all the bags in the bottom of your garbage pail, under the bag you're using. That way, they'll be right where you need them, when you need them. You can also buy storage dispensers for plastic bags that mount to a cabinet door with adhesive pads or screws.

DRY GOODS Boxed dry goods should be stored by type. Group breakfast cereals together, rice and beans together, and staples, such as flour and sugar, together. Bags of staples like dried beans, rice, and sugar are odd shapes for shelf storage. It's more space-efficient to store these in labeled airtight see-through plastic bins or storage containers.

DISHWARE AND GLASSES Store dishware and glasses on an accessible shelf in a cupboard as close to where you usually eat as possible. Store glasses in rows, so it's clear where they belong, and leave room around all your tableware so nothing gets broken when moving pieces in and out of the cabinet.

POTS AND PANS The first line of defense against pot and pan clutter is nesting: Whenever possible, store one pot inside a larger one to reduce the amount of space they take up. You may want to invest in a slide-out cabinet tray. A simple tray or bin can serve the purpose of collecting pot lids in one place. For roughly the same cost, you can buy a wire pot-lid rack that will keep them in a neat row.

Undersink Space ⏱ 15 MINUTES

The cabinet space under the sink, with its odd dimensions and intrusive pipes, can seem nearly unusable. But the space can actually be outfitted to provide for a range of storage; it's just a matter of choosing the right organizer for your needs.

To make the space as efficient as possible, create groupings under the sink. For example, keep all household cleansers in one container, such as a bucket or carryall. Do the same with poisonous household products. (Be sure to use a childproof cabinet lock in homes where children are present.)

PULLOUT STACKING-BASKET SYSTEMS You can take advantage of available space with a pullout system of tiered baskets. Easy to get at, they can be used to store most anything you would want to put under the sink.

UNDERSINK STRETCHABLE SHELVES Designed specifically to expand to the dimensions of undersink space, the best of these can be adjusted for both width and height. They provide fairly sturdy support for bottled cleansers, detergents, and other bulky items.

DOLLAR SMART

All in the Family: For a low-cost alternative to hanging bars in your kitchen, look to bath accessories. Basic towel racks with simple S hooks can serve as hanging racks in the kitchen. Short towel racks attached on the inside of cabinet doors can be used as lid holders.

SLIDE-OUT OR PULLOUT TOWEL BARS Simple chrome rods on runners or hinges are a great way to hide towels from view most of the time, while keeping them accessible.

CABINET-DOOR-MOUNTED RACKS AND TRAYS These allow for storage in handy places, such as on the inside of undersink cabinet doors. These small units range from wire or acrylic bins that can be used to hold sponges or dishrags to more complex, multicompartment tray systems that can store extra bottles of dish soap, scrub brushes, and other cleaning supplies.

ABOVE LEFT An undersink stacking basket system keeps cleaning supplies in order and slides out for easy access. ABOVE RIGHT Pullout towel bars make cleanup a breeze—the towels hang to dry out of sight between uses and are close at hand when they're needed.

TRAY DIVIDERS Undersink partitions are a great use of space for cooks with few cabinets who do a lot of baking with cookie sheets, griddles, muffin pans, and other long, flat bakeware. The dividers can be stationary, or you can purchase higher-end units with adjustable dividers fixed to a platform that slides out.

PULLOUT GARBAGE AND RECYCLING PAILS Some of the most useful undersink additions you can buy are dual bins mounted on smooth-action runners. They make taking out the trash or recycling so easy, it's almost a pleasure.

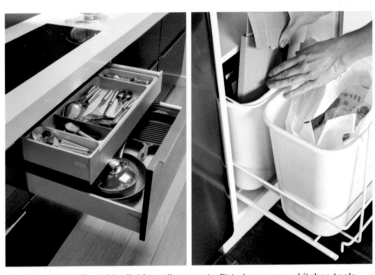

ABOVE LEFT Adjustable dividers allow you to fit twice as many kitchen tools in a drawer, and your equipment will stay organized. ABOVE RIGHT If you keep your trash and recycling bins close to one another, you and your family will be far more likely to sort properly. It makes things handy for you, and it's also good for the planet.

Hanging Storage | ⏱ 15 MINUTES

Much of what clutters cabinets and drawers can be hung from the ceiling or a wall. Both ceiling- and wall-mounted racks come as a simple unit, or a rack-and-shelf combination. Wall-mounted units allow more flexibility to accommodate your height and reach.

When considering hanging cookware or other kitchen necessities, look for unused wall space or areas of the ceiling over work spaces. It's best to avoid hanging items over or near the stove. Measure carefully, and don't hang storage where it will impede work flow or get in the way of cabinet—or refrigerator-door swing. Ideally, anything hung in the kitchen should be in arm's reach of the shortest person who will be cooking there.

Hanging rails can hold a full complement of storage accessories, from individual utensil hooks to a cookbook rack to small shelves for spices and condiments.

RAIL SYSTEMS Pick a hanging-rail bar and then select from a variety of accessories to create your own customized system. The bars are sold in different lengths, so you can make a system to fit available space. Accessories include:

- Bottle caddy
- Utensil hooks
- Book holder (to keep a cookbook open at eye level during food prep)
- Dish racks
- Paper-towel holder
- Shelf (available as a single or double unit)
- Corner shelf
- Hanging knife-block
- Cutlery holders
- Stemware racks

POT RACKS Hang pots, pans, oven mitts, towels, and more from these handy and fashionable units. Available in an array of sizes, shapes, and materials, pot racks can supply much-needed storage, freeing up a lot of cabinet space. They also look great and let you position pots and pans near where you will use them.

Pots and pans take up a huge amount of cabinet space, and it can be time-consuming to have to unstack your nested items. A hanging rack near your stovetop will allow you to reach exactly what you need when you need it. You can also store additional often-used equipment, like colanders and graters, nearby.

HANGING BASKETS Easily some of the most adaptable and useful hanging storage units, hanging baskets can hold many things, and they take up relatively little vertical space. Placed near a food-prep area, a three-tiered basket provides a place to keep fruits and root vegetables that are not refrigerated. By the kitchen table, a single hanging basket can hold colorful napkins and place mats.

HOOKS Ordinary hooks can be as useful in the kitchen as they are in other rooms.

- Hooks are good choices for places where hanging bars and racks won't fit.
- They work where you need to hang only one or two items, such as a dish towel, oven mitt, or a string of garlic or peppers.
- Hooks keep backpacks and jackets from collecting on the kitchen table.
- Specialized mug hooks for undercabinet storage can provide easy access to these often-used items.

HANGING GLASS RACKS Stemware racks vary in size, from small wall-mounted units that will support eight to twelve glasses to overhead units that can hold more than twenty. You can also buy units with a wine-rack shelf above the glass storage, though wine is best stored in a cool, dry place.

ZONE 4

Keeping your kitchen drawers organized is simple but essential to making the kitchen as efficient as possible. The key to keeping drawers neat and tidy is to limit them to storage by type. If you are using a drawer for phone-station storage, don't keep wine openers and serving spoons with the notepad, pencils, and takeout menus there. Keep flatware drawers free of large utensils. Segregating drawer storage makes it clear to anyone in the kitchen where items go, and more likely that every item will be put back where it belongs.

Most of your kitchen drawers are shallow. This makes them appropriate for storing flat items, such as linens, napkins, flatware, and cutlery. But you can adapt your drawers for many other types of storage with a little help from a drawer organizer.

ABOVE LEFT One of many drawer organizers available, this wooden insert turns a drawer into a handy spice rack with at-a-glance convenience. Before purchasing this type of organizer, be sure to count the number of spice jars you have in order to estimate the size organizer you will need. ABOVE RIGHT: A sliding top tray provides access to everyday flatware, while the bottom insert holds accessories and less frequently used utensils.

SPICE INSERTS These one-piece units have slots that hold spice jars at an angle, making it easy to see and grab what you need.

FLATWARE CADDIES They're the best way to keep your knives, forks, and spoons in order. Choose from wire, plastic, or fancier wood types. Just make sure you get a caddy that will hold all your flatware and still fit neatly within the dimensions of your drawer.

EXPANDABLE CUTLERY ORGANIZERS These units are used for the same purpose as flatware caddies, but expand to the size of the drawer and provide more varied storage slots for your steak knives and other cutlery and utensils, such as can openers, in addition to the space you need for your day-to-day flatware.

KNIFE RACKS If you don't want to hang knives and don't have counter space for a knife block, keep knives in order with a knife-tray drawer insert. These also keep the knife blades sharp by avoiding contact with other items and surfaces.

EXPANDABLE COMPARTMENT ORGANIZERS Adjustable in length and width, these cousins of expandable flatware organizers come with odd-size compartments to store everything from wine openers to twist ties to straws.

INTERLOCKING ORGANIZERS Individual clear or white plastic compartments can be assembled in any number of combinations to create a custom storage drawer.

ROLLING TRAY INSERTS These units provide two levels of storage for deep drawers.

KITCHENWARE ORGANIZERS If finding a good place to store your dishes is a problem, a kitchenware organizer may be the answer. You'll need a large, sturdy, deep drawer. The organizer features a baseplate with holes, and pegs that can be moved to accommodate different-size plates.

ANATOMY OF A JUNK DRAWER

Dissecting your junk drawer can be a revealing exercise that includes lessons for organizing the rest of the kitchen.

PAPERS

Aside from recipes, coupons, and a notepad to record calls and make shopping or to-do lists, the kitchen should be a paperless place.

- Throw away out-of-date documents (flyers, expired coupons, ticket stubs).

- Current coupons should be kept in an envelope or simple plastic wallet paper-clipped to the pad you use for shopping lists and phone messages.

- Notes you've made and phone numbers you've jotted down should be moved to your office, where they can be filed (except for an emergency phone numbers list, which should be kept in a plastic sleeve next to the phone or hung on the refrigerator with a magnet).

- Move takeout menus to your phone station (see Zone 5, page 31).

- Homework and other miscellaneous papers should be moved to their proper areas in the house.

UTENSILS

Utensils you use frequently should be grouped with other utensils in containers or in drawers. Duplicates and items you never use should be given away. Discard anything that is in bad shape.

OFFICE SUPPLIES

The only pens or pencils in the kitchen should be kept in the phone station. Backup notepads, sticky reminder notes, rubber bands, paper clips, and other work-related paraphernalia should be moved to the home office or work desk.

CHILD'S PLAY

Toys and other kids' stuff, such as pacifiers, bibs, and rattles, should be moved to the child's bedroom. If your children are grown, these items should be discarded or given away.

MEDICAL SUPPLIES

Most medicines should be kept in the bathroom, in the medicine cabinet. Medications meant to be taken with meals can be placed with your vitamins in a cool, dry place out of direct light, such as a kitchen cabinet. Bandages and gauze pads should also be placed in the bathroom. If you're concerned about kitchen emergencies, mount a first-aid kit on a kitchen wall so it's easy to find when needed. Make sure to position this kit out of the reach of small children.

HOME IMPROVEMENT LEFTOVERS

Screws, nails, small tools, and other home-improvement materials should be moved to wherever you keep the household toolbox. If you find that you frequently need to make small repairs to the same item in the kitchen, consider taking it to a professional or replacing it.

LOOSE CHANGE

Move loose change from the junk drawer into a container you keep in your bedroom, or wherever you empty your pockets every night. If you family has a policy of paying a fine when someone misbehaves (say, by cursing), choose a plain, tall vessel and place it in an unobtrusive corner. Be sure to cash in the contents when it is almost full.

Countertops, Work Surfaces, and Shelves

 15 MINUTES

So much of what is stored in the kitchen is attractive, and shelves and countertops give you a chance to use storage containers that double as decorative pieces.

Items stored on countertops and work surfaces should be confined in functional "stations." This will leave long stretches clear to serve as work surfaces whenever you need them.

PHONE STATION The ideal phone setup for the kitchen is a wall-mounted phone over accessible counter space. The phone station should include a "frequently called" number list with emergency numbers, a notepad, takeout menus, and a pen or two.

- If the station is next to the refrigerator, use a magnetic notepad with a pen on a cord and a magnetic pocket to keep menus and other papers organized.

- If the refrigerator isn't close, use a tray near the phone, and keep notepad and papers confined to the tray.

WORKSTATION FOR COOKING Clustering basic implements and ingredients you regularly use in cooking can make meal preparation quicker. Self-contained units do the trick here. Keep often-used utensils on a lazy Susan, with compartments for cooking oil, salt and pepper, and basic condiments. Position commonly used staples such as garlic and onions next to the food-prep workstation.

OPPOSITE The central island in this well-equipped kitchen serves as a food-preparation workstation. A centralized work space keeps the mess in one place and makes cleanup a breeze.

FOOD STATIONS Group staples in containers. For example, a countertop group of airtight canisters holding sugar, flour, coffee, and tea keeps these frequently used consumables centralized and accessible. You can create container groups of dried beans, grains and cereals, and oils and vinegars.

SMALL-APPLIANCE STATION Unless you use a small appliance almost daily, find a place to store it off the countertop or work surface. Essential appliances, such as coffeemakers and toaster ovens, will need to be positioned near outlets. Whenever possible, buy models that mount under upper cabinets. This makes it easier to keep the counter clean and organized.

OPPOSITE Wall-mounted shelving provides open display storage for your serving pieces and everyday dishes. ABOVE This countertop coffee station is hidden away behind an undercabinet fold-down door when not in use. Appliance "niches" allow for a streamlined look.

TV STATIONS If you like to have a TV in your kitchen, find a corner where the set will take up as little space as possible. Better still, opt for a small, fold-down undercabinet model that can be kept out of the way when it is not being used.

Shelves are available in all shapes and sizes. Buy shelving according to your needs and available wall space. Although chrome wire shelving is popular, consider wood, solid metal, or plastic shelves if you need storage for tall, thin containers; they will be unstable on wire shelves.

STAND-ALONE SHELVES An independent unit can be a quick fix for lack of storage just about anywhere in a kitchen.

- Tall, thin shelving units can fit in the awkward wall space between two doors, or between a door and a window.

- Short, wide units will be handy if you need to store heavy items, such as mixers, blenders, and other large appliances.

- Anchor taller units to the wall with screw-in braces.

WALL-MOUNTED SHELVES These types of units are best for "overflow" storage.

- If you have too many canned goods for available cabinet and pantry space, install a shelf near the pantry for extra storage.

- Use shelves for more immediate needs; in the case of canned goods, use the shelf rather than the pantry for foods likely to be consumed most quickly.

- Simple, solid shelves are also a good place to put cookbooks and other kitchen reference materials.

If you have the room, an "accessory tree" can provide flexible storage. The pole can hold a number of shelves, which can be positioned exactly where you need them.

Refrigerator and Freezer 30 MINUTES

Keeping your refrigerator organized is one of the bigger challenges in the kitchen. You can maintain order by being diligent about where things are put, and by establishing a logical organization within the refrigerator. (Be sure to tell family members your organization principles so they'll abide by them.) The first order of business is weeding out obviously spoiled foods and leftovers. Then throw out any opened jars, bottles, or cans that are more than 6 months old, and anything else that you haven't used in recent memory. You'll need to do the same weeding out in the freezer. If you have food in the freezer that is more than 9 months old, throw it out. Now give the whole unit a thorough cleaning and you're ready to put everything back according to assigned locations.

PACKAGED FOODS

- Use transparent covered bins for bags of food, such as shredded cheese.
- Keep bottled condiments together in the door shelves.
- Other packaged foods, such as ground coffee, should be kept together in trays—these will contain spills and make it obvious what goes where.

This lazy Susan is ideal for refrigerator storage. Made of easy-to-clean plastic, the molded lip contains spills, and the small size is perfect for making crowded refrigerator shelves more accessible. Rotating the unit allows you to grab what you need without having to reach.

THE REFRIGERATOR RULES

1. CONTAINERIZE. Collect loose food items (such as open packages of lunch meats and shredded cheeses) in containers. Each container should be dedicated to one food type and clearly labeled. Vegetables are an exception; they should be kept loose in the crisper.

2. ASSIGN SHELF SPACE. Assign different types of food (such as dairy or prepared meals) to their own sections of the fridge. If you have a large family or a large fridge, use labels so everyone knows which area is which.

3. ROTATE. Whenever you put a new item, such as a carton of milk, in the refrigerator, move any already opened items in front so that the older one is consumed first.

BEVERAGES Soda bottles have a tendency to tip on wire shelves, so if your refrigerator has them, buy a piece of Plexiglas at the local hardware store (have it cut to size) to serve as a platform for soda bottles and other tall, unsteady containers. Canned beverages should be organized in a wire can-dispenser. If you're a fan of sports drinks and buy several bottles at once, refrigerate only one at a time—keep the rest in another location, such as the pantry.

LEFTOVERS You should also have a distinct area for leftovers so you and your family know where to find them.

A prefab shelf system can be the ideal way to turn an alcove into a spacious pantry. All the shelves and drawers in this installation are adjustable, allowing the design to change along with your needs.

Pantry ⏱ 30 MINUTES

A pantry is your kitchen's warehouse. It lets you stock up on staples and provides a dedicated location for backups of common household items, from extra boxes of coffee filters to a supply of paper towels. If you're fortunate enough to have a built-in pantry as part of your home, the challenge is to make sure it's well organized. But even if a pantry isn't part of your home's layout, you can usually create a pantry space in your kitchen. To prevent clutter and waste, there should be a logic to what you put in the pantry and where you locate it.

DRY GOODS Airtight bags of flour, sugar, rice, tea, and other dry foods in bulk are well suited for storage in the pantry. As a space-saving alternative, use airtight containers that fit your shelves perfectly.

PAPER GOODS Even though backup items generally go on bottom shelves, position paper goods close to the top of the pantry so they can't be damaged by random spills or crushed by heavy items.

BEVERAGES Most beverages can be stored in a cool, dry pantry space for a significant period of time. This frees up refrigerator space and lets you buy beer and soda at case prices. Keep the beverages in their cases for most efficient storage.

COOKBOOKS Because the pantry is usually set apart from the working area of the kitchen, it can be a perfect place to store cookbooks. If you don't have a pantry, keep the most frequently used cookbooks handy in the kitchen and move the rest to bookshelves elsewhere in the house.

There are many ways to fabricate a pantry, from putting adjustable shelves or a freestanding shelving unit within a closet to buying one of the many prefab pantry systems. Whether you make your own or buy a ready-made pantry system, look for flexibility, such as adjustable shelves. You should be able to change the configuration of the pantry based on your changing storage needs.

A pullout, wire-grid storage system lets you convert a ceiling-height cabinet or a small broom closet into a new kitchen pantry.

- Individual shelves can be arranged to accommodate items of different heights.

- You can also buy accessory grids designed to hold pot lids and utensils.

- You can opt for pullout, solid trays that will hold many different containers firmly in place.

ABOVE LEFT Turn a tiny broom closet into a full-service pantry with this space-expanding wire-shelf system. Easy to install and to keep clean, it slides out on runners. ABOVE RIGHT Keep a busy kitchen well stocked with a stand-alone pantry. This piece of furniture has amazing capacity with its swinging doors and pullout compartments. When shut, it looks like a set of cabinets.

THE PANTRY RULES

1. TAKE STOCK. A pantry should be used as backup storage so that you have extras of everything you need on hand.

2. ORGANIZE BY LEVEL. The order of items on pantry shelves depends on how often you need them. Long-term storage of backup items goes on bottom shelves. The most commonly used dry goods should be placed at eye level. Items that are rarely used go on the highest shelves, out of everyday reach.

3. NO PERISHABLES. Pantries should be used for dry goods and staples with long shelf lives. Foods that might spoil in a few days need to go in the refrigerator or near the food-preparation area.

ZONE 8
Kitchen Table 15 MINUTES

Your kitchen table provides multiple uses, from a social center to a place for eating meals to a desk for reading. Because so much goes on around the kitchen table, clutter is a natural problem. You can beat clutter by "centerpiecing" whatever is stored on the table and by keeping the table ready for meals.

Centerpiecing is simply creating a central area—on a small lazy Susan or with some other type of small organizer, such as a basket—where all the items that will be permanently kept on the table are collected and organized. Put the basics—salt, pepper, napkins—in the centerpiece, leaving a small amount of space for other condiments used during mealtime. Use bowls around this centerpiece, as necessary, to keep fruit or other treats on hand for the family.

Keep the table covered with a simple tablecloth or lay out place mats, and you'll be able to keep the table free of the clutter of homework and bills.

Maintaining Clutter-Free Kitchens and Pantries

Even after you've put all your organizational changes in place, you'll need to remain vigilant to the accumulation of clutter. Use these strategies to ensure that clutter doesn't become a problem again.

1 Empty sink, closed doors

Make a habit of emptying the kitchen sink every night and closing all open cabinet doors. These simple acts make clutter on counters and cabinets stand out. Deal with this clutter every night; a quick pickup is far easier than tackling a big cleaning.

2 Weekly bin run

Keep a small decorative bin or tray on a shelf or counter near the table. Each night, put anything that doesn't belong on the table in the bin. At the end of the week—or when the bin is full—whichever family member has the most items in the bin must empty it by putting everything back where it belongs. After a few weeks, everyone will want to avoid the responsibility of emptying the bin, and they will all see the upside to keeping the kitchen table clutter-free.

3 Fridge weeding

The inside of your refrigerator can too easily become a case of "out of sight, out of mind." Assign 1 day every 2 weeks for fridge weeding. Remove and discard leftovers, fruits, vegetables, and dairy products that are past their prime. Then make sure that the oldest items are placed in the front of the refrigerator, and that you're sticking to the other guidelines in Zone 6.

CHAPTER 2

Bedrooms and Kids' Rooms

BEDROOM ZONES

1 Closets
2 Bedside and Bed
3 Dresser
4 Suspended Storage—Hooks and Shelves
5 Accessory Furniture

KIDS' ROOM ZONES

1 Toy Storage
2 Work-Art Space
3 Bed-Play Area
4 Clothes, Closets and Dressers
5 Book Storage
6 Special Storage

A bedroom is all about comfort and seclusion. A highly functional space, it's where you dress and get ready to face the day. But no matter what you're doing in your bedroom, it will be easier, more enjoyable, and more refreshing if the space is neat and orderly.

The most obvious source of clutter in the bedroom is clothing. Your clothing changes over time with the seasons and the whims of fashion. But your closet space and the way it is organized often do not change. This means that much of what you wear probably doesn't have a proper place in your closet, or is stored haphazardly. The result can be an alarming jumble of clothes. The solution lies in reorganizing the closet to accommodate what actually needs to go there, and moving what doesn't.

Bedroom furniture and accessories also play a part in how easy it is to dress or undress without leaving a trail of clothes. Something as simple as a well-organized jewelry box with separate compartments for earrings, rings, and necklaces can make dressing quicker. It will also keep the top of your dresser clutter-free. Used effectively, your bedroom furniture can provide short- and long-term storage, and can free up much-needed closet space.

Organize the zones in this room in this order: closets, bedside and bed, dresser, suspended storage (hooks and shelves), and accessory furniture. When considering the times listed for each zone, realize that they take into account a two-person bedroom. If you are the only person using your bedroom, you can expect to spend less time on each zone.

OPPOSITE This simple, cozy bedroom uses a few wisely chosen furnishings. The trunk at the foot of the bed provides additional storage to keep the space organized.

Furnishing a clutter-reducing bedroom means limiting where things can be put. This simple bedroom includes smart furniture and accents that beautify while they simplify.

1

A mounted reading light saves space on a nightstand.

2

This nightstand is ideal for a streamlined bedroom; having no drawers and a tray top limits what can be put on it. A vase, an alarm clock, and a picture fill the space nicely.

3

The modest bench is useful for laying out tomorrow's clothes, and as a surface for a folded blanket or two. The minimal area and slotted surface fight clutter, too.

You should be flexible about where things go, letting common sense and practicality guide you. Creating an appropriate mix of storage areas, and making the most of those areas, will go a long way toward maintaining the bedroom as your own orderly sanctuary. In addition, always be sure to put magazines, mail, photos, and so on in their proper zones in other rooms; don't leave them strewn about the bedroom.

ZONE 1
Closets 🕐 1 HOUR

Your bed may be the centerpiece of rest and relaxation, but your closet is the cornerstone of bedroom organization. Fortunately, closets are fairly easy to organize, and there are many products available to help you do just that.

You can choose from a long list of innovative closet-organizing accessories. These include shoe-cubby shelves, specialized multi-garment hangers, belt racks, revolving tie-racks, wall- or pole-hung canvas shelving, and more. You can also opt for a completely new, customized closet system, designed by one of the many companies specializing in closet organization.

The first step in making the most of your closet is assessing the space. Remove everything in the closet and measure the dimensions. You'll use these measurements to determine what kind of storage should go where, as well as for purchasing any type of closet-organizing system or elements.

Next comes the shedding process. Go through what you've removed and weed out the clothes you have not worn in the past two to three years, as they will not likely be worn again, and remove anything in the closet that is more logically stored elsewhere, including clothes that are out of season. Now you're ready to organize what remains.

A busy professional couple requires a well-organized closet, and this design meets their needs admirably. A variety of hanging storage options is augmented with shoe cubbies, shelves, cabinets for oversize items, and abundant drawers.

STORAGE IN STYLE

Basket Case: So much of what you need to store in the bedroom is soft and easy to fold or roll, which makes baskets a natural choice for keeping things tidy. Baskets also make beautiful display containers that let you keep all kinds of garments out in the open. Use wicker or reed baskets to hold rolled towels or folded sweaters. Use smaller woven baskets for scarves and gloves.

HANGING STORAGE Try to limit the amount of clothes that will be hung, because folded clothes take up less space.

- Most pants—even dress slacks—can be carefully folded.

- Button-down shirts can be folded; this makes it easy to see the shirt you want and keeps them in a neat stack.

- Decide which garments absolutely must be hung, such as business suits and blouses, and group them by how much hanging space they'll need—long or short.

Now you have a good idea of how long each closet rod must be. Look to optimize your hanging storage (while being careful not to overload the rod with too much weight for the supports you are using). If you have extra space on a closet rod holding long dresses and bathrobes, use a "stacking hanger" with several bars to hold a number of pairs of pants in limited horizontal space. Avoid rod-mounted tie or belt racks and hanging shelves; it's usually wiser to reserve hanging space for clothes on hangers.

SHELVING Closet shelves should always be adjustable to allow for changing storage needs. Anything you put on shelves should be grouped with like items—all sweaters together, all shoes in a row, and so on.

- Wire shelving is widely available in preset widths, and is usually sold with matching brackets or as part of a complete closet system. Wire shelving can also be cut to your desired width. This type of storage is fairly inexpensive and is fine for holding boxes and other flat items. However, wire construction may leave lines on folded soft clothing, and will allow loose objects to fall through. Often, the better choice is laminate or wood shelving.

- Laminate shelving comes in a range of set widths and depths, and is supported on tracks that let you move the shelves as needed. Wood shelves offer a nicer look, and can be cut to suit specific measurements. If you are going to stack clothes, such as sweaters or pants, use enough shelves in the column to ensure you don't stack more than three or four garments on a pile. (Clothes stacked higher are apt to slide or fall off the pile and become messy.) For ultimate convenience, choose plastic or laminate shelves that slide in and out of grooves cut in the side supports.

Tall piles of soft clothes have a way of tipping over and getting jumbled. A simple set of stacking shelves can help keep soft clothes organized and avoid unnecessary wear and tear on your garments.

THE INSIDE SCOOP

Fenced Off: Long shelves can easily fall into disarray as piles of clothes or shoes become jumbled together over time. Consider using a partition on long shelves. These accessories clip or screw onto the shelf, dividing the shelf into compartments that contain different items in their own spaces.

CONCEALED STORAGE Depending on the size of your closet, you may opt to include drawers or pullout trays for organizing smaller items. A drawer for a closet is usually shallower than one for a dresser and is mounted on the same vertical brace that holds the hanging poles (or on brackets, like other closet fixtures). Most closet drawers have dividers to create separate compartments within the drawer. There are also many specialized drawers available with compartments specifically designed to hold handkerchiefs, scarves, stockings, socks, belts, and so on. If you can include as many drawers in your closet as you need, you may be able to do without a regular dresser, freeing up space in the bedroom.

SHOE STORAGE Shoes can create chaos in the closet.

* A quick, easy, and inexpensive solution is a simple wire shoe rack. This keeps shoes up off the floor and slanted at an angle so you can quickly find the pair you want.

* You can also keep shoes on shelves.

* If you're installing a complete closet system, choose a cubbyhole shelf with slots for each pair of shoes. Store each pair of shoes heel to toe, making it easier to see and grab the pair you want.

- Alternatively, you can put shoes in canvas or plastic hanging shoe-holders. Different types can be mounted on a wall, a closet rod, or the back of a door; they allow you to simply slip pairs of shoes in and out of the pockets. For the easiest access, keep shoes grouped together based on use (for example, dress shoes with dress shoes, casual with casual, and so on).

THE INSIDE SCOOP

Hanging Around: When clothes are given the appropriate amount of space in the closet, they are easier to remove and replace, making dressing and undressing easier. The right amount of space also keeps the clothes wrinkle-free and reduces unnecessary wear and tear. The proper horizontal spacing lets you easily pass your hand between garments hanging next to each other. Here are general guidelines for the vertical space you should allow for different clothes (measured from hanging bar to top of surface below it, such as the floor, another hanging bar, or a shelf):

45 inches Suits, dress shirts, blouses, sports jackets, other jackets

35 inches Trousers folded over hangers, ties

70 inches Dresses, gowns, bathrobes, trousers hung full lengths

DOLLAR SMART

The Versatile Shoe Box: Empty shoe boxes are assets that can save you money you might otherwise spend on fancy organizing boxes. Shoe boxes can be painted, stenciled, or decorated to fit in with your bedroom decor. The storage space can be used for any number of loose goods, from bras to scarves to art supplies. Draw a label on the outside, or take a photo and tape it to the front so you know at a glance what's inside the box.

Hooks are a simple, economical way to free your closet from bulkier items like tote bags, bathrobes, and sweaters. You can find them in a variety of styles, and they can be affixed to almost any surface.

DOOR STORAGE Sliding doors don't provide any storage opportunities. But if you are willing to replace sliding closet doors with hinged double doors, you'll increase the storage potential of the closet. A variety of organizers can clip onto the top of swinging doors to add storage on the inside surface:

- Over-the-door closet rods provide more places to hang clothes.
- Utility racks can support many different types of clothes (from hats to coats to shirts on hangers).
- Shoe racks.
- Tie racks.
- Simple multipurpose hooks.
- Hinged, foldout hanger-racks let you hang a column of pants flush against the door.
- Dowel racks attached to the inside face of the door let you position your tie or purse collection at eye level.

BORDER PATROL Sharing closet space—even with a loved one—can be a trying experience. As you organize your closet, create a border between your storage space and your partner's. The border can be the vertical board that holds the support for hanging rods or a column of shelves. If one of you has more clothes and needs more space than the other, organize that side first.

THE CLOTHES QUESTIONS

When it comes to your wardrobe, the more streamlined the better. To make sure the clothes you have are the clothes you wear, ask yourself the following questions:

Is the article more than two sizes too big or too small? If so, you should give it away. The drastic change your body would have to undergo for the clothes to fit properly will likely take months, if it happens at all.

Has it been more than a year since you wore the piece? Older pieces often don't match new clothes we buy. These "orphans" just don't fit with your wardrobe, so donate them. You won't miss them.

Upon close inspection, are the clothes in bad condition? Even clothes that fit look bad on you if they are threadbare. If you've found worn or frayed areas on a garment, discard or donate it.

Have you changed careers or left a line of work? If so, you may have perfectly nice (and expensive) clothes that you no longer need and won't be wearing. Donate them to charity.

THE CLOSET RULES

1. HANG LESS. Many of the clothes you are in the habit of hanging up can be stored folded, taking up far less space. Folded items can be placed in a range of locations, including shelves out in the open, closet shelves, drawers, and bins and baskets.

2. BE FLEXIBLE. Because your clothing requirements change throughout the seasons, your closet should have as many flexible features as possible.

3. GROUP BY TYPE. Keep similar clothes together—dress shirts with dress shirts, jeans with jeans, and so on—and they will be easy to locate when you want to wear them.

Bedside and Bed  30 MINUTES

The territory around your bed—including the bed itself and your nightstands—is your comfort area. If you're a reader, there should be a place to put books or magazines when they're not being read, and enough room for a good reading light. If you like to sleep with the scent of flowers around you, your nightstand surface should be large enough to hold a vase of blooms.

We tend to think of our furniture as permanent, but if your nightstands are too large or too small, they are part of the clutter problem and should be replaced. However, the problem may lie in what you are trying to keep in or on the nightstand.

NIGHTSTANDS Your needs should determine your nightstand, not the other way around. The right nightstand will work well with your bed and the other furnishings.

- The top surface should be easy to reach from the bed height. If your nightstand is too tall or too short, it will make basic tasks, such as setting your alarm or turning a reading light on or off, more difficult.

- If the nightstand is too large, it will invite clutter, and if it's too small, the basics you need won't fit comfortably on top. Ideally, the top of the nightstand should be large enough to hold a book, a light, an alarm clock, possibly a vase, and eyeglasses, if you require them.

- The nightstand should also have a drawer to conceal items that would detract from your bedroom décor, such as prescription medicines, a television or stereo remote, and a small flashlight.

- If you have a number of medications or other items you use while in bed, consider a nightstand with multiple drawers.

The small surface area dscourages clutter, and the single drawer and shelf allow you to keep necessities nearby.

A guest bed with built-in drawers leaves plenty of room for visitors' clothing, making a dresser unnecessary.

- A shelf underneath is useful for holding magazines and books. Be sure to cycle them out when you finish reading them.

- If an item is not used while you are in bed, it doesn't belong on or in the nightstand.

THE BED All beds—except completely solid platform models—provide the opportunity for valuable long-term storage. There are a number of ways to put the space under a bed to good use.

- First, determine what type of long-term storage you need. Bulky items like comforters need a taller container than flat, compact items such as sheets.

- Measure how much clearance you have between the bottom of your bed and the floor, then choose a type of underbed storage that suits the space and the degree of accessibility you require. For example, backup pillows and sheets that you use every few weeks might best be stored in a short container with wheels so you can get to them easily.

- Depending on which type of underbed storage you choose, you may want to use a bed skirt to conceal the container.

STORAGE IN STYLE

Excess Baggage: You can put your luggage to work even when you're not traveling. Use traditional case luggage as underbed storage containers for seasonal clothes and bed linens, such as flannel sheets. For real flair, pick up vintage luggage at yard sales, thrift shops, or flea markets, clean it well, and use it as underbed storage.

Base drawers are prefab units that slide independently under the bed or create a foundation for the box spring or mattress. They are usually attached around the existing frame. Most often made of wood, these units create the appearance that your bed is sitting on a platform with drawers. The drawers provide a neat, finished look that stylishly conceals what you're storing. The downside to under-bed drawer sets is their cost and the fact that the frame construction takes up some of the usable underbed storage space.

Simple underbed boxes are inexpensive storage options. These come in a range of shapes and materials, including durable plastic boxes that let you see the contents, wire-mesh units that allow air to circulate around whatever you're storing, and simple canvas "bags" that zip up around a metal or wood frame, completely enclosing and hiding the contents.

Rolling boxes and trays are ideal for storing those things that you need to use more often, such as sweaters. Choose from rolling plastic containers with casters and snap-shut lids, stylish wicker boxes on wheels, open wire-mesh units, and rolling plastic frames with sliding drawers.

One of the many types of underbed storage boxes, this plastic shoe organizer zips completely closed to keep out dust and dirt, and slides neatly under the bed.

ZONE 3
Dresser ⏱ 30 MINUTES

The dresser provides two types of storage: concealed places to hide underwear, socks, and other clothing and valuables, and an open, accessible top surface for a jewelry box, family pictures, or other visually attractive elements. The challenge is to make certain the dresser does not become the parking place for the random clutter that seems to migrate to the bedroom, such as mail or car keys.

This dresser unit is a part of the closet system. It helps fight clutter by keeping all clothing in one area.

Small loose items can make a mess of a dresser top. Even a simple dish can provide a handsome gathering spot for your keys, watch, and other small items.

Begin by removing everything in and on top of the dresser.

- Weed out frayed undergarments that you no longer wear, socks and handkerchiefs with holes in them, and other garments that are no longer usable.

- Get rid of small bits and pieces that you might have been holding on to for no good reason, such as orphaned cuff links and earrings.

- Move items that don't belong in the dresser, such as playing cards or sunglasses.

What's left will be a combination of clothing and possibly items of value that have no other logical place to go. That's okay. The dresser should serve as a central storage area for garments, and can also house valuables—like medals and awards— that you want to keep but won't necessarily be using or even looking at on a regular basis. The trick to permanent dresser organization is to give everything that goes in or on the dresser a set place, even if you have to create one with special dividers or independent compartments, such as boxes or trays. Then put back all the clothing you'll store in the drawers, which will reveal how much extra storage space you have.

Built-in dividers create uniform compartments in this drawer, ideal for ties or rolled-up dress socks.

DRAWERS As with the closet, all the clothes you keep in the dresser should be neatly grouped by type. If much of what you want to store is loose goods, turn to drawer inserts. Specialized inserts are available for everything from earrings and necklaces to rolled ties and folded handkerchiefs. You can also mix and match independent plastic or wood compartments. Some plastic compartments snap together, letting you customize your drawer design.

DRESSER TOP Whatever is on top of the dresser should be self-contained.

- Jewelry should be kept in a jewelry box.
- Cosmetics should be placed on a decorative tray or in a box or cosmetics bag to prevent them from migrating.

ABOVE LEFT A pretty tray organizes and confines disparate objects, like a collection of perfume bottles with different shapes and sizes. ABOVE RIGHT Jewelry tray inserts make a jewelry box out of a dresser drawer. Lined in velvet, they prevent jewelry from scratching and keep it organized in various sized compartments.

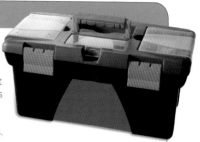

Jewelry Storage: Organizing the bits and pieces of a jewelry collection is always a challenge. A small plastic toolbox can be ideal—the many different shapes and depths of the compartments let you separate pieces so they remain untangled and easy to pick out. For an even simpler solution, use ice-cube trays.

- A valet—as formal as a wood tray with separate compartments or as informal as a woven basket—will conceal all small "pocket" clutter: cell phone, keys, money clip, wallet, and anything else you regularly carry.

- A change keeper is the place to put all your loose change when you empty your purse or pockets. This can be a decorative bowl, a vintage bank, or even a wide-mouthed bottle.

- The point is to create a set place for all the loose items that might otherwise clutter the top of the dresser.

If you have small children, be sure that your dresser has safety straps to secure the dresser frame to a wall stud, along with safety catches on the drawers.

Suspended storage is all about "hiding in plain view." Because so much of what you need to store or organize in the bedroom is pleasing to the eye, using hooks and shelves can be your chance to organize and decorate at the same time. When you use shelves and hooks, you free up room elsewhere in the bedroom, and make whatever you store easier to find.

You can choose between complete stand-alone shelving units and single shelves that are attached directly to the wall. Hooks come in sets, alone, or in functional variations, such as pegs. Always keep in mind that flexibility is key to how useful any storage—including shelving units—will be.

STORAGE IN STYLE

Cube-ism: A great way to add hidden storage with flair is to mount cube shelves—square shelves made from four pieces of wood that form a frame—on a wall and cover their openings with fabric flaps, such as canvas, muslin, or velvet. The flaps are attached with top hinges. Choose a fabric that complements your bedroom's décor, or paint or stain the fabric to suit your design tastes.

STAND-ALONE SHELVING Independent shelving units offer a lot of storage space in one unit. They can also easily be moved when necessary, and are a good choice where you have significant wall space. Organize anything you put on a shelf by type (books in a group, boxed items in a group, and so on).

ATTACHED SHELVES Single shelves and brackets are available in just about any finish you could want, from metal to wire to all kinds of wood and plastic. Although an attractive choice because of their price, wire shelves tend to look inexpensive, and will let small objects pass through. A solid shelf is usually a better idea in the bedroom. Position the shelf near where what you're storing will be used. You can prevent loose articles from falling off the end of the shelf with a shelf-end stop. This device clamps to the end of the shelf and creates a border like a bookend.

OPPOSITE Increase the capacity of closet shelves quickly, easily, and inexpensively with undershelf bins that slide right into place.

HOOKS Useful and versatile, hooks serve as either permanent or temporary resting places for bedroom garments and accessories.

- Hook sets comprise a series of hooks attached to a backing, which is hung on a wall. These are useful when you're hanging a group of similar items, such as all your scarves, purses, or belts.

- Single hooks are simple solutions that can easily be installed right where you want them: on the back of the bedroom door for your bathrobe, on an interior closet wall to hold a favorite pair of suspenders, or next to the dresser to hang the necklaces you wear most often.

- Peg sets are helpful, too. For example, you might install a row of pegs at the top of a wall, but within reach, to create a display of baseball caps.

Accessory Furniture 30 MINUTES

Depending on the size of your bedroom, you may have room for other furnishings. Any additional piece of furniture should have a distinct purpose to avoid becoming clutter itself—it should never interrupt the traffic flow through and around the room—and to avoid becoming a clutter magnet.

CHESTS AND TRUNKS Not only are they interesting additions to the room's décor, chests and trunks also provide useful long-term storage.

- Choose a style that suits your tastes, from an old steamer trunk to a contemporary cedar hope chest.

- Let size guide your selection. If you want to store thick blankets, look for a deep chest with no auxiliary compartments or inserts.

- If you are storing frequently used guest linens with seasonal sweaters, look for a trunk with a tray or other compartment to separate the two types of storage.

- The lid of a chest or trunk also provides a resting place for more frequently used items, such as bathrobes or books, or you can use it as a place to sit while dressing.

- Of course, only include a chest or trunk in the room if you have genuine long-term storage needs; decorative chests have a way of collecting clutter.

CHAIRS AND TABLES If the bedroom can accommodate it, a good reading chair is a lovely addition. Keep the chair in a corner out of the flow of traffic. Along with the chair, you may want a small table. The table should only be large enough to accommodate a book and a cup of tea. Use a good standing lamp and your reading area will be complete.

OPPOSITE Chests and trunks provide attractive long-term storage for extra blankets or even seasonal clothing. Placed at the foot of the bed, as shown here, a sturdy trunk can also provide convenient seating. ABOVE A little bedroom desk nestled in a small alcove next to the bed provides a place to read, write, and keep a log, with drawers to manage keepsakes.

- Entertainment centers: Although your home entertainment area should ideally be confined to a family or living room, you may opt to create a small entertainment center in your bedroom. If you do this, keep it as contained as possible.

- Try to position the TV and peripherals, such as audio equipment, in a recess (on a shelf) so that their top surfaces don't become a place for more clutter.

- Secure cables to baseboards with nail-in clips to keep them out of the way.

- Use a remote caddy or similar dedicated container for your remote controls so they don't get lost between pillows on the bed or slide down between the dresser and the wall.

- If you have a laptop computer in your bedroom, designate a shelf or drawer for storage when it's not in use.

DESKS The zone system calls for keeping any desk in a separate home office. But a small desk positioned in the bedroom may be more convenient for your purposes.

- Try to keep the top of the desk as pristine as possible; that way, any clutter that finds its way to the desk will stick out like a sore thumb.

You don't need a large bedroom to accommodate all the furnishings you want. A streamlined desk provides enough space for working, and a small chest of drawers eliminates surface clutter.

- If the desk has drawers, use them to store simple writing implements and to hold other items that would normally crowd the top of the desk.

- Use a chair that will slide all the way under the desk so that it is out of the way of traffic flow and won't become a parking place for clothing.

Maintaining Clutter-Free Bedrooms

Because of the relaxed nature of a bedroom, it's easy to allow things to slowly become disorganized again. A little periodic maintenance goes a long way toward a spotless, comfortable bedroom.

1 Culling closets

Every 3 months or so, do a closet check. Remove older items that you no longer wear, or that were replaced by new additions to your wardrobe. Reorganize garments by type if they have gotten mixed up in the process of cleaning and rehanging or refolding.

2 Drawer check

Once each month, right after you do the laundry, take a minute while you're putting away underwear and socks to ensure that your dresser is as organized as it should be. Are like items grouped together? Is it simple to find exactly what you need? Are there any loose items on top of the dresser that need to find a home? Straighten up, as necessary, to keep the dresser a functional, tidy zone.

3 Bedside scan

Get in the habit of making a weekly visual sweep of the bed and surrounding area. Remove anything that shouldn't be there, and make sure your nightstand is as neat and organized as it was when you first finished the zone.

Kids' Rooms

The term "kid's room" has several different meanings, depending on the age of the child. Obviously, the décor and organization of a toddler's room will need to be different from a teenager's, but certain basic principles are fundamental to organizing any child's room.

The key to helping children keep their rooms in order is the way you integrate storage and organization aids into the design of the room. Just putting a laundry hamper and toy box where kids can see them isn't going to do it.

The more the process of organizing is innovative, interesting, and part of a daily routine, the more likely children will be to make the effort to stay organized. This can mean purchasing interesting storage solutions, thinking up novel approaches to avoiding clutter, and even letting kids come up with fun organizing and storage solutions as part of a creative exercise.

The storage solutions you pick should be as flexible as possible, and they should be safe. Because your child moves quickly through stages and ages, whatever you use as storage in a child's bedroom should be adaptable. For example, using real wood chests that can be repainted and repurposed as your child grows is often a more economical option than a less expensive, molded-plastic, cartoon-character toy chest. The solutions suggested in this chapter are adaptable to a range of ages.

Although the zones presented here cover elements in most kids' rooms, one or more may not be applicable to your child's room. For

OPPOSITE This toddler's room has a tall dresser with abundant storage and a high surface the child can't reach—or lay toys on. The toy chest has safety hinges and all-wood construction that ensures it can be redecorated and reused as the child grows.

This teen girl's room proves that a kid's room can be hip and orderly. The steel locker-type pieces can be stripped and repainted for later use in a rec room, garage, or an adult's bedroom.

1

A workstation provides a dedicated place for homework and room for a small computer setup. The keyboard sits on a platform that slides out of the way and the chair rolls under the desk, keeping the whole unit as contained as possible.

2

A handy place to sit is combined with storage. The unit is made more convenient with casters. The drawers can store folded clothes, jackets, and blankets.

3

A simple dresser offers
plenty of room for
folded clothes. A set of
decorative glass vases
discourages the place-
ment of loose clothing
on the dresser.

4

Deep underbed stor-
age provides a place
for extra comforters or
blankets, or for collect-
ibles or toys the child
wants, but does not
play with anymore.

example, art and play areas may be one and the same in your son or daughter's room. So pick the zones that apply to your child, and tackle them in an order that makes sense for you. Note that the times listed for each zone reflect an adult organizing the zone. If you are working through the process with a child, you'll naturally have to set aside more time. Start with the messiest area, and work from there. Including your child in the process by bringing in fun, creativity, and innovation may make straightening up your child's room easier on both of you.

ZONE 1
Toy Storage ⏱ 30 MINUTES

Young kids love their toys. Given the diversity of sizes and shapes, the amount of small removable pieces, and frequency of use, it's no wonder that toys are the largest source of clutter in any young one's room.

The first step to getting toys in order is winnowing out broken toys, safety hazards, and those the child has outgrown. Try to do this with your child: You may be surprised at what he or she no longer wants to keep.

INFANTS If you have an infant, you're in control of the toys. But that can become quite a chore because so many people give toys as gifts. Don't be afraid to donate toys that never get played with or are stored in closets. Create a "favorites" bag for the small toys that your child likes the most. You can use a backpack or any other fabric bag with a loop or handle (even a mesh laundry bag will work). Fill the bag with the baby's favorite toys and move it wherever the child goes—to the playpen, changing table, stroller, and beyond. Because infants make a mess of things within their reach, keep extra stuffed animals, learning toys, and toys for later ages together—by type—on a high shelf or in a box with a latch.

TODDLERS TO PRETEENS Beyond the age of 2, children's toy collections become increasingly diverse and extensive. Keeping the growing population of toys in line requires a variety of storage solutions.

Benches, boxes, and chests can provide ample storage to accommodate an assortment of toys.

- If you use a toy box, consider buying one without a lid or removing the lid from the one you have. That way the child sees exactly where the toys are supposed to go, and can literally throw them in there. It removes one step in the process—that of opening the lid—making it much easier to stay organized. It also removes the possibility of the lid closing on small fingers. If you keep the lid on, look for boxes with finger cutouts and lid-control devices with safety hinges.

- Bench toy boxes serve two purposes: seating and storage. Find one with a slatted lid so it's easy to see the toys inside.

STORAGE IN STYLE

Toy Pockets: Recycle an art apron with clear pockets or a plastic hanging shoe bag as easy-to-reach containers for small toys, from baby rattles to army men to Barbie accessories. Simply hang the apron or shoe bag by hooks (or over a door if it has hanging brackets) within the child's reach. As your kids grow, they can change what's kept in the pockets.

ABOVE LEFT A large basket, with a picture of the toy that belongs inside, makes it easy for toddlers to help clean up. ABOVE RIGHT Multiple baskets keep different types of building blocks together and prevent a messy jumble in a toy box.

Bin consoles are great solutions for rooms with more than one child. These are essentially groups of stacked cubes with pullout baskets.

- The cubes can be self-standing or mounted on a wall, but it's always better to keep things low so that small children can get to what they need without being tempted to climb on them.

- Toys in consoles can be grouped by type or by child.

- Some consoles come with simple transparent boxes that let the child see what's inside.

- Other units have wicker or wood baskets that can be labeled with words, a picture, or an icon (for example, you can attach a small stuffed bunny to the front of a basket containing stuffed animals).

- Choose a stylish, well-made bin console and it will serve your child from the crib through college.

A mix of toy storage options keeps any play space neat and orderly. This child's room includes a large toy chest, large standing shelves, and a wall-mounted shelf; all can be repainted for use in just about any room in the house when the child gets older.

Shelves are ideal for board games, puzzles, and "collections" of toys.

- Dedicating a shelf to one type of toy ensures that your child is very clear about where that type of toy goes when it is not being used.

- Board games and puzzles should be placed on shelves that leave plenty of room for new games.

- If the games are usually played with the entire family, move them to where there is more available space, such as a shelf in the family room.

ABOVE LEFT Making storage apparent helps children see where things go. This inexpensive wire-cube unit can be reconfigured to suit the child's storage needs and the space available. It can be freestanding or wall-mounted, and the cubes accommodate a range of items, from books to toys. ABOVE RIGHT Novelty hampers provide amusement and a clutter solution. This one has hooks to hang conveniently on the back of the door. The basketball version encourages shooting until the clothes are "dunked."

TEENS Many teens opt for high-tech forms of entertainment. Chances are your son or daughter has plenty of gadgets, such as a mobile phone and/or handheld device, a video game console, an MP3 player, and possibly his or her own computer. These types of devices need a safe place to stay when they are not in use to ensure they don't get lost or broken.

- If your teen's room includes a computer, keep portable music players and handheld game consoles in a padded tray or box nearby. It's best if this container has a drawer or enough extra space for batteries and any other peripherals, such as the cord that connects the music player to a computer, and chargers.

- If the room doesn't have a computer, keep the box or tray near where your teen listens to music, such as a homework area or bed.

- Use heavy tape and permanent marker to label chargers, and keep them coiled up and secured with binder clips when not in use.

STORAGE IN STYLE

Handy Hamper: Woven fabric or wicker laundry hampers can serve as great toy keepers for bigger kids (the child needs to be able to reach down into the bottom). They can be painted to suit the child's taste, and can be painted again later and used once more as a hamper when your child gets older.

Net Gain: Create a quick and easy toy catchall that will serve your child from infancy through the preteen years. Simply buy a mesh toy "net" that attaches in the corner of a room. The net creates a hammock to hold soft toys, such as stuffed animals. Or make your own toy net with three screw-in hooks and a mesh laundry bag or mesh child-safety gate. Just place two of the hooks on perpendicular walls, and a third near where the walls meet in the corner. Then attach the netting like a hammock, allowing it to form a pouch in the middle.

Work-Art Space ◯ 1 HOUR

Encourage your child's creativity by creating a real art area. You don't need a lot of space, just enough for a small desk or table, a light, a chair or bench, and a little spot for art supplies. This can also function as a work area where your child can do homework or school projects as he or she grows. Obviously, the space will need to expand as your child grows into his or her teen years. High school art and science projects tend to take up more room than homework assignments from earlier years. Preteens and teens will also use different equipment—most notably, computers.

A simple, inexpensive art table for small children can host hours of fun. This one includes storage bins as end supports and built-in rollers for rolls of art paper.

FURNITURE The work-art space will need to change as your child grows older, so you should choose furniture and organizers for their adaptability.

- If you decide to buy an easel for your child, you might want to spend a little extra for a wood unit with telescoping legs that can grow as your child does.

- A secondhand drafting table can be lowered or raised to accommodate children of different ages.

- If you are hoping to use a piece such as a desk for the entire time the child lives at home, consider first how the desk will be used when the child is older (younger children require less space). A teen is likely to need space on a desk for textbooks, a computer, a monitor, and—possibly—a printer.

A self-contained art wardrobe is an ideal piece of furniture for the creative preteen. Offering plenty of room to work and store supplies, the desk can be folded down and out of the way—and the wardrobe closed—when not in use.

SUPPLIES Art supplies can be used by children young or old. Keep them organized so they are less likely to get lost, damaged, or destroyed.

- An all-in-one art kit is a good idea for any child, and you can make your own from drawer organizers arranged in a large, clear plastic box.

- Teen artists will need enough room to slide a full-size art portfolio behind a desk or against a wall.

- As your teen begins to specialize in an art form, the supplies he or she uses will likely be self-contained, such as a case that holds sketching chalks.

ARTWORK Finished artwork, from finger paintings to clay sculptures, can become clutter. The way to organize finished artwork is to display it or store it.

Two-dimensional artworks, such as painted pictures and sketches, are easy to display.

- Pin them up on a corkboard or frame them with an inexpensive frame from an art store. Save these pieces in a three-hole binder (if they can be punched without damaging them), an oversize folder with pockets, a small hanging-file box, or an underbed plastic box.

THE INSIDE SCOOP

High-wire Act: Use a thin cable (available at home centers and hardware stores), clothesline, or length of sturdy twine to make a gallery display of your child's sketches or paintings. String the cable or twine between two walls and hang the artwork with binder clips or clothespins. Make sure your child signs his or her pieces!

A bin console provides easy, accessible storage for art supplies, clothes, toys, and more. Choose one with bins that pull out. The rugged plastic types here are durable and easy to clean, and the unit can work in the pantry, garage, or crafts room when your child outgrows it.

STORAGE IN STYLE

Fantastic Plastic: Recycle plastic containers with lids (like margarine tubs) and plastic jars or wide-mouthed plastic drink bottles for your children's art supplies. Bins and tubs can be used to keep individual jars of paint in order, and for storing other loose art supplies. Use taller containers for loose brushes, pencils, and crayons. Your child's first art project can be decorating these containers.

Stuck Up: Buy Velcro strips in packs at home centers or hardware stores (they come in regular and heavy-duty varieties—get the one rated for the weight of what you will be hanging). Stick a series of strips on the wall to hold fuzzy stuffed animals or larger toys to which you've attached a mating strip. You can even put a small piece of mating strip on the underside of jacket collars so kids can hang their jackets on the Velcro wall!

- Have your child draw or paint on thepages of an oversize art pad. Display the child's favorite piece by opening to that page and leaning the pad against the wall. After all the pages are used, store the pad on a shelf or in an underbed container with other treasures.

- You may opt to let the child decorate the entire room, creating his or her own gallery of artwork. As the child creates new pieces, you can rotate the work on display.

Three-dimensional art, such as papier-mâché masks or molded clay figures, should be displayed on high shelves in order to prevent breakage. If you are storing three-dimensional art, use hard plastic or wood containers with straw or foam packing material to keep it safe.

THE ART AREA RULES

1. KEEP CLEANUP GEAR CLOSE. A supply of paper towels, moist towelettes, or rags makes it more likely that accidents will get cleaned up promptly.

2. USE APPROPRIATE SUPPLIES. Kids' art supplies should be nontoxic and water-soluble. Never bring home professional-quality paints or supplies for young children's art projects.

3. CONTAIN CREATIVITY. Store all art supplies in cleanable containers in the art area. Use recycled plastic containers for disposable purposes, such as mixing paints. Explain to kids the need to put away clay and put lids on paints to keep supplies fresh.

Bed-Play Area   1 HOUR

In a child's room, the bed and play area are usually one and the same. Younger children incorporate the bed into their play, from using it as a stage for make-believe to creating pillow-and-blanket forts. Older children, such as tweens and teens, continue to consider the bed an extension of their recreation area. They use it as a place to read, listen to music, and talk to their friends. The trick is to provide enough storage and organizers to keep things tidy around the bed without letting those additions become part of the problem.

BEDSIDE TABLE There's only one person in the bed, so there should be only one bedside table (unless, of course, there are two children in the same room).

- Just as with an adult's bedside table, a child's needs to be easily reachable from the bed—neither too tall nor too short.

- A child's nightstand should be more modest than an adult's. There can be a shelf underneath the top of the nightstand, but don't include a drawer, because it will invite a disorderly collection of loose objects.

- Keep in mind that—children's motor skills being what they are—anything on top of the nightstand is liable to fall to the floor at one time or another. Consider using a clip-on lamp or one with a plastic base.

- There should be enough room for a book or two, a lamp, an alarm clock, a phone in the teen years, and not much else.

- Because children so often put things down without thinking, limit the number of surfaces on which they can just set things down.

BED A child's bed generally has less room underneath than an adult's, but there is still enough space for significant underbed storage.

- Commit to some sort of underbed storage. Otherwise, this space is likely to become cluttered with in-line skates, stuffed animals, and various papers. Underbed organizers send the message to kids that the space is not to be used as a place to hide things.

- A rolling box or tray is ideal for board games, clothes that you are waiting for your child to grow into, collections of artwork, or other long- or medium-term storage (for more on underbed storage, see pages 59–60).

Bunk beds have their own requirements. Because the sleeping areas are stacked, only one child will have access to the nightstand, but the child on top of the bunk still needs the storage space of a nightstand.

- Put up a small shelf for books and toys.

- Hang a lamp on the ceiling or wall, within reach of a child lying on the top bunk.

- Use a hanging basket as a nightstand of sorts for the top bunk.

PLAY TABLE If the room is large, a play table can go a long way toward keeping the whole area in order.

- The play table should be big enough for children to play a board game on, but not so large that it impedes traffic flow.

- The best kind of play tables is about as high as a coffee table and has a safely hinged top with a compartment underneath.

- Remove the table when your children reach their teen years— they probably won't use it, and replacing the table will eliminate one more surface that can gather clutter.

OPPOSITE This child's bed makes it impossible for underbed clutter to gather. The built-in drawers provide an easy-to-reach spot for clothing, and organized bins are perfect for storing toys.

This vanity is perfect for a teenage girl—the surface is small, so she can't keep too many items on it, and the many small drawers allow her to store makeup, hair-care items, and more.

TEEN DRESSING AREA As children grow up, they become more conscious of their grooming habits. This is especially true for tween and teenage girls. At some point, your daughter may want to convert part of the play area into a space for a vanity.

- A small table with a mirror and room for a makeup kit will usually suffice.

- Make sure your tween or teen has a box that will hold all her makeup and grooming supplies, so that these don't become clutter in other parts of the room.

THE INSIDE SCOOP

Easy Illumination: Consider using battery-operated "touch lights" for young children who get up in the middle of the night or want to read before sleeping. These inexpensive round lights mount on a wall or other flat surface, and are turned off and on by simply touching the face. They come in a range of decorative face covers, such as moons, stars, and other fun designs. These are an especially good option for children sleeping on the top bunk of a bunk bed. You can also buy more conventional lamps—both wall-mounted and desk lamps—with bases that children can turn on and off just by touching.

Tent Control: Kids love a "fort" of any kind, and today's indoor play tents are understandably a big favorite. But a tent can quickly become a clutter zone. Give your kids a small fabric bag (even an old purse or tote bag will do) and tell them that toys can go through the tent door only when carried in the "tent keeper." If the keeper is inside the tent when kids are playing, they must bring it—and the toys that went in with it—out, before anything else can go into the tent.

Clothes, Closets, and Dressers

 1 HOUR

Children's wardrobes require different storage and organizational tools. The closet is where this difference is most glaring. Not only do the clothes have to be accessible to the smaller stature of children, but clothes in a child's closet are also going to be rotated in and out frequently as the child grows. The closet setup will also have to change radically when children grow into their tween and teen years and pay much more attention to their wardrobes.

Dirty clothes present another challenge in a kid's room. Whether in the closet or out in the open, a child's laundry should be stored as close as possible to where he or she undresses. Try to make using the bag or hamper as fun and interesting as you can. Put a basketball hoop over the top of the opening, or mount a target on the wall above the laundry bag.

THE CLOSET There are two key principles behind designing a child's closet to promote organization and fight clutter.

- First, the focus needs to be on easy access and intuitive location.
- Second, the closet will have to change as the child changes. The most blatant example of this is a closet hanging rod. Look to eliminate hanging rods in your young child's closet. Even if he or she has dress clothes, those clothes are so small that they can easily be laid flat in a drawer or on a shelf. (Where you don't have a flat surface large enough for a child's dress clothes—such as a boy's jacket—you will need to hang them.) As your child matures into adolescence and through the teen years, he or she is going to need more hanging storage (although still not as much as you require).

OPPOSITE A teenage girl's closet reflects the need for stylish storage. Varied hanging storage holds dresses, skirts, and shirts, while a column of sleek mesh baskets keeps folded clothes and accessories in order. A set of plastic compartments turns two mesh bins into storage drawers for small loose items.

The better choice for most children is a closet comprising shelves and drawer units. If you're leery of giving up all hanging storage, buy a wire shelf unit with a hanging bar incorporated into its construction.

- Organize shelves by type of clothing, using attached shelf dividers, as necessary. This will make it clear to children what goes where, while showing them how organization works.

- Use closet shelves and drawer units with brackets that allow complete repositioning.

- Drawers used in a child's closet should be transparent plastic or wire mesh so that the child can see what's inside.

- Use simple wood or wire-mesh units for shoes, and add extra units as the child's shoe collection grows.

STORAGE IN STYLE

Magazine Bank: Children and teens love to collect issues of their favorite magazines. Keeping those loose-bound volumes from spreading all over is easier than it may appear. Either buy plastic magazine "library boxes" or make your own. Use an overnight delivery box or a cereal box, and with the box standing on its base, remove the top and cut one of the narrow sides of the box from top to midpoint, spine to spine. The opening will let kids see which issues are stored, and the box will keep the magazines in order.

THE INSIDE SCOOP

Hang Two: If you prefer to use a hanging bar for your young child's dress clothes, make sure the clothes are within the child's reach. Hang a bar from the existing closet rod. Simply tie two 6-foot lengths of clothesline or nylon rope to form two loops around the existing rod. Then slide a rod made from a cut-down broomstick, round wooden stick, or lightweight pipe through the bottom of the loops.

With a little planning, an infant's closet can be arranged to hold almost all of the child's clothing, bedding, towels, and accessories.

THE DRESSER A dresser is the closet overflow in a child's room. Ideally, you should buy a three-drawer wooden changing table that can be used for your infant, converted to a dresser as your child becomes a toddler, and then repurposed for your teenager.

- For infants, use dividers to organize drawers by type of clothing or type of cleanup aids (wet wipes and washcloths in one section, onesies in another, socks in another).

- With toddlers, try to keep just one type of clothing per drawer. To help your toddler learn where clothes are, attached a picture of a shirt or pair of pants to the front of the drawer that holds those clothes. Be sure to secure a child's dresser with safety straps to avoid accidental tip-over.

- In the teen years, help your child keep organized by using drawer dividers. Make sure the drawer divisions reflect how your teen actually dresses. For example, he likely uses T-shirts as undergarments, has other T-shirts to use as everyday outerwear, and has a third group for special occasions such as concerts and going out. Each type should be in its own place in the dresser.

Preteen and teen girls may want a place for makeup and other beauty products. A foldout cabinet with mirrors keeps brushes and other grooming supplies in one area.

A modest dresser is fine for young children. This small three-drawer unit holds the folded clothes of a young boy. As he grows, the dresser can be repurposed as a nightstand.

THE KIDS' CLOTHES RULES

1. ORGANIZE LOW TO HIGH. What children wear every day should be within reach. Use high shelves and hard-to-reach areas for long-term storage.

2. AVOID THE HANGER. Kids, even teenagers, find hangers a hassle. If you want to get them to keep their clothes organized, avoid the hanger as much as possible. Most of what kids wear can be hung on hooks or pegs, or folded and stored on shelves or in drawers.

3. SPELL IT OUT. Even young children can be trained to put away clothes where they belong, especially if you use a device such as having pictures taped to the front of the appropriate storage area for children who can't read, and funky-colored labels for those who can.

4. LAUNDRY ENTERTAINMENT. To ensure that kids get in the habit, make putting dirty clothes in the hamper fun. For small children, make a large clown face out of cardboard, with a big hole in the mouth, and put the face over the hamper.

Reading to infants is a great way to bond, toddlers can begin to learn their alphabet by looking at board books, and older children choose the books that they want to read. But all books need to be kept in good shape to be enjoyed.

That's why books should never be put into a toy box, where the spines are likely to get broken and the pages dislocated. A bookshelf is an essential piece of furniture in any child's room.

A standing bookshelf is preferable to a wall-mounted shelf, because children—even older ones—tend to be careless in their movements, and a wall-mounted shelf may fall after being bumped one time too many. Standing bookshelves represent adaptable space in a kid's room: If you have more space than books, you can always use the extra space for storing boxes of baseball cards, dioramas, or the latest science project. Use a low, wide bookshelf to keep the books within the child's reach and to discourage climbing. Always anchor standing bookshelves to a wall with safety straps.

A simple standing bookshelf with four compartments lets you organize books by type, or you can use some of the space for toys and games.

Special Storage 🕐 30 MINUTES

A few specialty products can help kids keep their lives organized with a minimum of fuss and effort.

A backpack hook can help keep your child focused on his or her studies (and keep the backpack clean and neat in the process). Attach a hook near the door to the room. Before the child can hang the backpack on the hook—where it's supposed to go—he or she has to empty the contents. This will prevent forgotten homework assignments that would otherwise be balled up at the bottom of the backpack. It also avoids the mess of a week-old, half-eaten sandwich or a rotten, squashed banana.

Hanging organizers are the best use of a closet rod—and they can also be hung from the top of a door or the bottom of a wire shelf if you've removed the rod. These organizers are made up of canvas columns of compartments that can be used to store a wide range of items, from clothes to shoes to stuffed toys. They are especially useful for helping kids store clothing, school gear, and other important items neatly.

- Label each compartment in the organizer with a day of the week. Small children can keep each day's clothes in the compartments so they're ready to go in the morning.

- Older kids can use the organizer to keep homework assignments straight, school projects in one place, and the right gear or musical instruments ready for the day they're needed.

Maintaining Clutter-Free Kids' Rooms

Maintaining your child's room as a clutter-free environment is easy once you involve your child. There are many ways to get your child into the organizing habit.

1 Toy patrol
Every night, as part of the bedtime ritual, your child should put toys back where they belong.

2 The pickup path
If children—from young kids through teens—can't walk directly to their bed from the door, they need to pick up whatever is in their path and put it where it belongs.

3 Weekly visits
Once a week, make sure the storage in your child's room is being used correctly. Make a checklist of problem areas and give it to your child. Giving a child a checklist is much more effective than saying "clean your room," because checklists provide defined goals, not vague ones. After a few checklists, most children (beyond the toddler years) learn to periodically do their own inspections.

ZONES

The bathroom is one of the busiest spaces in the home, so it doesn't take long for it to become overrun with wet towels, dirty clothes, and empty shampoo bottles.

The battle to prevent all this clutter is made more challenging because of the confined dimensions of any bathroom. But you can actually use the space limitations to your advantage. It's fairly simple to organize and position necessities close to where they will be used, so they can easily be put back.

Introducing order to this hectic room is a matter of tailoring solutions to the number and type of people using the bathroom. (The times listed take into account the needs of a family of four. If you're the only person using the bathroom, you can expect to cut those times in half.)

- In a woman's bathroom, the issue may be the need to find effective storage for cosmetics and personal care products.

- If one or more children are using the bathroom, it's important to establish a place for bath toys and dirty clothes.

- Men require some sort of organized station to deal with their daily grooming needs.

- The family bathroom faces all these challenges, plus organizational challenges, like tissues, toilet paper, cups, medications, towels, and more.

But don't be discouraged. Follow the zones, in order, and you'll have more bathroom storage than you have ever thought possible, organized in a way that will make the space easier to keep clean.

OPPOSITE Instead of stuffing the linen closet with clean towels, roll them up and store them under the sink. In this bathroom they're easy for a busy family to access, and they provide a decorative touch.

INSIDE SCOOP

Smaller Is Better: Limit the size of your bathroom wastebasket to keep things tidier. A smaller wastebasket gets emptied more often, and it's easier to notice if something has accidentally fallen into the trash. As in the kitchen, keep a few plastic trash bags (or old supermarket bags) at the bottom of the wastebasket to encourage easy and frequent disposal.

ZONE 1
Medicine Cabinet ⏱ 30 MINUTES

A medicine cabinet is an amazingly useful feature. It's the ideal place to keep all those small everyday items used in the bathroom—from toothpaste to eyedrops to prescription medications (stored according to manufacturers' instructions)—well organized and out of view.

But precisely because the storage is hidden and handy, a medicine cabinet tends to become the "junk drawer" of the bathroom.

- The first step in any bathroom organization effort is to remove everything in the medicine cabinet and give the cabinet a good cleaning.

- Now look at what you've removed and throw away empty containers or products that are not used regularly.

- Properly discard old medicines—both over-the-counter and prescription—that are past their expiration dates. (Check with your local poison control center for recommendations on how to discard expired medicines.) Be aware that even herbal remedies and "natural" products, such as melatonin, carry expiration dates. Remember, too, that all medicine cabinets and drawers in households with children should be equipped with a safety locking device.

- Now organize what's left by use. For example, put everything having to do with dental care (floss, toothpaste, mouthwash) in one area of the medicine cabinet.

- In some cases, what you would normally want to put in the cabinet won't fit. An economy-size bottle of mouthwash may be too big to stand upright, so you'll need to store it elsewhere. Find a smaller bottle or flask with a tight-fitting top, fill it with the mouthwash, and keep it in the cabinet.

- If you have limited sink-top space and no nearby shelves, you may want to keep your toothbrush in the cabinet as well.

INSIDE SCOOP

Built-on Option: Some bathrooms are equipped with a wall-mounted mirror instead of a built-in medicine cabinet. But that doesn't mean you have to do without the handy storage a cabinet provides. Surface-mounted cabinets are simply attached right to the wall over the sink. Although these are shallower than built-in units, they still provide a wealth of accessible storage and only take about 30 minutes to install. You'll find an excellent selection at large home centers.

Sinks and Vanities | ⏱ 1 HOUR

The area around your sink provides a place to put everyday items near where they will be used. The vanity that holds the sink often includes abundant storage for the many things that wouldn't fit into a cabinet or even on a shelf. If you're thinking of installing a vanity, the customized storage options are amazingly diverse. Even if you're working with an existing unit, you can adapt it for a multitude of specialized storage needs.

Organize this zone from top to bottom, working from the sink top down to the drawers (if the vanity has them) and finish with the undersink cabinet space. Whatever you keep on the sink top should be kept in one of the storage options outlined below, in order to keep clutter in check. The same is true of the undersink space. Choose storage options that serve your needs, but make sure everything you store is contained in some way.

Keep in mind that any door or drawer a young child can reach needs a safety latch.

TOP SURFACE This is where you keep personal-care supplies and equipment you use every day, as well as decorative items. Whatever you put on the surface should be contained.

- Rather than laying your toothbrush next to a cup, use a toothbrush holder set with a matching rinse cup.

- Better yet, use a simple toothbrush holder and add a paper-cup dispenser to your sink top or wall. The improved hygiene will be well worth the extra cost.

- Limit cosmetics to the makeup you use every day. Other products should be stored in a drawer.

- You can also use a cosmetics carousel or vanity valet to organize your makeup in style. If you don't want to spend the money on an item like this, keep your makeup corralled in a basket, decorative bowl, or a stylish plastic zip bag.

- Men's shaving products are preferably kept in the medicine cabinet, although you can keep them on the sink top in a razor-and-shaving-cream caddy.

- Keep hand soap near the sink, but use liquid soap in a dispenser. Bar soap, even when it's in a soap dish, tends to get messy quickly.

- If you keep your hairdryer and hair-grooming tools on top of the vanity, put them in a hair-care organizer that will hold the dryer, brushes, and combs in their own compartments.

- Organize hair-care products in a separate tray or bin.

ABOVE LEFT Beating clutter on the sink top means keeping all loose items contained, and this unit does the job by corralling toothbrushes, hand soap, and a rinse cup in one handy unit. ABOVE RIGHT An attractive sink-top carryall keeps canisters and loose items under control and can be moved to where is most convenient.

Built-in undersink shelves are another
excellent way to organize a space that is often
left unused or in disorder.

DRAWERS Vanity drawers can be handy for storing some of what might otherwise clutter your surfaces. In fact, drawers represent an opportunity to organize often-used supplies, such as cosmetics, while still providing quick and easy access. How you organize your drawers is going to depend in large part on what you need to store in them.

Jewelry might find its way into your bathroom if you accessorize as the final phase of getting ready in front of the mirror. If you put your jewelry on in the bathroom, you should have a drawer dedicated to keeping it in order. Use preformed plastic or wooden jewelry inserts to keep everything tidy, or go with a more inexpensive option, such as muffin trays or rows of votive candleholders. Each different type of jewelry should have its own container. Just be sure to keep your jewelry away from water, which can cause corrosion, rust, or discoloration.

Makeup is easily organized in drawers. First, go through all your makeup and throw out anything that has expired (see "The Inside Scoop" on page 113). Then create a makeup organizer. Because of the variety of shapes and sizes, custom plastic compartments that snap together are excellent for keeping cosmetics in order. You can also use a flatware caddy to hold makeup brushes, bottles of nail polish, and other beauty aids.

Towels and washcloths can be stored in the drawers of larger vanities. Special tilt-down drawers provide plenty of space for folded or rolled towels, or even a bathrobe.

STORAGE IN STYLE

Lip Sink: Store lipstick standing up to better view the labels. Place a thin layer of florist's foam in the bottom of a decorative tray or box, then punch holes using one of the lipsticks so the tubes can be stored in rows, standing on end. Now they create a unique sink-top display, making them easy to see and use when you need them.

UNDERSINK AREA This can be an awkward storage space, given the presence of pipes, but the height and depth make it useful for storing many larger bathroom items—from cleaning tools to backup supplies. The undersink area is also a good place to conceal those things you don't want to leave out in the open, such as a toilet brush, a plunger, and some personal care products. The best way to turn the space into effective storage is to use some sort of divider, such as shelves or stacking bins. Organized properly, the undersink area can become the pantry of the bathroom. But without storage containers, it will become a messy, cluttered area.

Door racks can be mounted on the inside of vanity cabinet doors to hold magazines and packaged personal care products. These are available as simple plastic grids that form pockets for flat items, or

ABOVE LEFT Optimize a vanity with small organizers that provide storage for specific items and make the most of open undersink space. This handy rack is hung from the inside of the vanity door and keeps a curling iron, hairdryer, and hair-care products in one easy-to-reach place. ABOVE RIGHT Slide-out bins make the most of undersink space, providing a place for toiletries and bathroom supplies. This unit is freestanding, so it doesn't require any installation.

more complex wire structures with separate storage compartments to hold items of different shapes and sizes.

Baskets and specialized buckets keep bathroom cleaning supplies collected in one place. You can choose from simple plastic mesh baskets or go with more complex buckets, with handles and compartments for different types of cleaning supplies. If you have a lot of supplies or equipment to store, consider a sliding rack. The best have multiple tiers of adjustable storage and sit on smooth, gliding runners that provide the ultimate in access to undersink storage.

Undersink shelves can be sized and positioned to suit the space and most are adjustable. Special shelving units clamp onto and hang from the pipes, for efficient use of the space. Choose shelves based on what needs to go under the sink. For towels, you can use wider, inexpensive wire-grid shelves. For heavier supplies, such as bottles of rubbing alcohol, mouthwash, and other personal care products, use sturdy, bin-type shelves.

THE INSIDE SCOOP

Cosmetic Aging: Makeup has a life span, and you should only store cosmetics that are safe and usable. As a general rule, keep everything as tightly sealed and free of contaminants as possible to extend the life of the product. Throw away makeup if you notice odor, color, or texture changes. Here are time frames for discarding makeup:

Mascara	3 months
Eyeliners and shadows	6 to 8 months
Foundation and concealer	6 to 8 months
Nail polish	2 years
Lipstick	2 years
Compact powder	2 years
Powdered blush	2 years

Shower and Bath 🕐 30 MINUTES

Although the shower stall and bathtub have little existing storage space, it's easy to beat clutter in this area with just a few innovative organization aids.

BATHING AND HAIR-CARE PRODUCTS Organize these everyday essentials in a wire or plastic storage container; otherwise, they will just clutter up the edges of the tub or shower surround.

- Use one that can comfortably hold all the hair-care products you and others in your household use, along with a loofah, a washcloth, and any other personal care products you use in the shower (which may include shaving supplies for both men and women).

- Pick a smaller two- or three-shelf container if your needs are modest.

- You can select models that attach directly to the tile, either with special mounting hardware or with suction cups.

- For a simpler option, turn to caddies with hooks that hang from the showerhead stem. Make sure you buy one with the features that match the way you shower.

- If you use bar soap, you'll need a unit with a soap dish.

- If many people use the shower, you'll probably be better served by wide corner baskets on a tension pole. The pole is secured between the ceiling and the tub lip, and usually comes with three or four triangular basket shelves. Some even include a suspended no-fog mirror for shaving in the shower.

- If you regularly use a washcloth, be sure any shelving units you buy have a hook, or buy a separate suction-cup hook.

STORAGE IN STYLE

Pocket Purpose: Store children's bath toys in an innovative way: Use novelty "pocket" shower curtains positioned inside out. With the pockets on the shower side, the toys are easy to reach and create a fun look. Punch small holes in the pockets—if they don't already have them—so water can drain.

TOYS It's a simple matter to keep toys contained. Just pick an organizer that is large enough for all the toys (and then some) and can survive being waterlogged.

ABOVE LEFT Organizers such as these keep all your shower supplies in one place. The shower-neck hanging rack keeps shampoo and other personal care products out of the way, but within reach. The suction-cup holder can be stuck anywhere that is convenient within the shower. Both have ample compartments for different sized bottles and hooks for utensils, such as scrubs, brushes, and razors. ABOVE RIGHT Kids are more likely to use organizers that inspire their sense of fun, making this mesh toy bag a winner in the tub. The suction-cup attachments allow you to place it at the child's level during bathing, ensuring that toys get put back at the end of bath time.

- The container can be a plastic bucket or bin, but needs to have holes in it so toys can drain after play. Keep it on a mat under the sink.

- If you don't mind having the toys around at all times, keep them in a mesh shower-toy bag with suction-cup mounts. These range in style from simple net bags to elaborate organizers with cartoon characters. The advantage of these types of toy holders is that you can rinse the toys off in the holder after play, and then just hang it up to dry on the wall.

- You can also buy hanging organizers that drape over the lip of the tub and can be hung elsewhere to dry out after bath time. These are great for holding toys, children's shampoo, and grooming aids such as brushes.

STRONG ATTRACTION Adhesive magnetic strips or screw-on magnetic plates are a great way to store metal objects used every day, like nail clippers or tweezers. Buy strips or other magnetic fasteners at home centers or hardware stores, and mount them wherever you do your personal grooming.

INSIDE SCOOP

Dispensing Wisdom: If many people use the shower, you might consider a hotel-style dispenser for liquid body wash, shampoo, and conditioner. These types of dispensers keep the shower and tub area more orderly. Choose from a single molded unit with three refillable chambers, or three decorative, matching bottle dispensers grouped in a single bracket.

Toilet Storage 1 HOUR

A cramped bathroom requires that you look to the area around the toilet for storage. Although this may seem an unlikely region, you'll find a diversity of storage containers designed to take advantage of the odd spaces around a toilet. To start with, the toilet tank provides an accessible, flat surface. The thin gaps between toilet and vanity or toilet and tub are also adaptable for storage. The wall above the toilet is fair game as well. To truly defeat bathroom clutter, carefully assess how much storage you need in addition to what is already available in the medicine cabinet, sink, and undersink areas.

TANK TOP You may have thought that the tank top was useful only to hold a box of tissues or an extra roll of toilet paper. Think again.

- You can purchase a "tank-top caddy" to hold a number of small items, such as nail clippers, that might otherwise clutter the sink top.

- You can also employ hanging tank bags, small fabric caddies that are draped over the top of the tank like saddlebags. These are best used for magazines, but can also hold personal care supplies.

SIDE STORAGE In the bathroom, it's important to look everywhere for additional storage, including the slim spaces between the vanity cabinet and toilet, and toilet and bathtub. Manufacturers look to optimize these areas with storage containers ranging from the simple to the complex.

- A basic magazine rack will fit.

- If you have no other place to keep extra rolls of toilet paper, you can use a tissue stand or a more complex toilet paper–roll dispenser. These range from basic chrome poles over which extra rolls are placed, to sleek vertical columns that conceal the toilet paper, dispensing one roll at a time.

- Toilet brushes and plungers can be completely concealed next to the toilet in handsome chrome or colorful plastic holders.

- For smaller goods and supplies, you can use a thin "trolley" organizer, which is essentially a set of skinny drawers on wheels. These units roll right into the space next to a toilet.

ÉTAGÈRES AND SHELVING Before you choose between an étagère or shelves, decide how much extra storage space you need, and whether you would prefer exposed or hidden storage.

- Étagères—also sold as "space savers"—are essentially one-piece cabinet or shelving units, with extra long legs to stand on either side of the toilet tank. These units offer more storage than shelving does, and give you the option of using cabinets, shelves, or a combination of the two. Select from a remarkable diversity of styles, including chrome, wood, wicker, plastic, and combinations of these with glass shelves and cabinets. All bathroom étagères are built to allow clearance for a person to sit down or get up from the toilet. The same is not true of all shelving.

- Be sure to buy shelving made specifically for the bathroom, and always measure to prevent buying shelving that sticks too far out. Some of the best shelves for bathrooms are glass, because the material isn't harmed by the vast changes in temperature and moisture to which a bathroom is regularly subjected, and the surfaces are easy to clean. You can opt for coated-wire shelves, but they are far less attractive and small objects tend to fall through. Finished wood shelves and plastic are two other reasonable options.

OPPOSITE LEFT A slim tower adds storage using the often overlooked space between the toilet and the vanity. Slide-out drawers keep supplies at hand and the streamlined design will fit in with most bathroom décors. OPPOSITE RIGHT A simple étagère provides a wealth of enclosed and open storage in the "dead zone" over a toilet. The frosted glass cabinet adds a touch of sophistication and a place to conceal private items.

Walls, Doors, and Floor Space

 **① 1 HOUR**

Finding the maximum amount of storage in the bathroom requires looking at all surfaces as potential storage areas. In a bathroom with ample square footage, you'll want to use a portion of the floor for additional freestanding storage. In more compact bathrooms, extra storage can be found on the walls or even the back of the door.

TOWEL STORAGE Options for towel storage are wildly varied. Alternatives to a simple straight towel bar abound.

- Pick a multitier towel bar for a bathroom used by a large family.

- Choose a towel ring for smaller hand towels and where wall space is at a premium.

- Combine storage types by installing a combination towel-bar-and-shelf.

- If you live in a part of the country that experiences cold winters, look for heated towel racks so you can step out of the shower and wrap yourself in a toasty towel.

- Roll towels into tight tubes and stack them on a shelf to store more towels in a small space.

- Rolled-up towels can also be stored in unconventional containers, such as wall-mounted terra-cotta planters.

- You should put up hooks or pegs for used towels to dry on.

- Folded towels can be stored on just about any flat surface, including a cabinet top or a wide shelf. Stack towels with the folded side out to make it easier to remove the one you want.

- If you have abundant floor space, you can even treat yourself to a standing towel-and-robe valet.

MOUNTED CABINETS AND SHELVES To display or not to display? That's the main question you need to answer when deciding between wall-mounted cabinets or shelves. With the range of products available, you'll find a shelf or cabinet to fit in just about any space you might have. The one other factor that may affect your selection is door swing. If the bathroom is especially narrow, you'll want to limit your options to shelves or cabinets with sliding doors. Always measure the maximum dimensions of what you want to store before buying a cabinet.

A multipurpose shelf unit provides plenty of open storage, a towel bar, and cubbies that segregate useful decorative containers. The wood construction can be painted or refinished to suit the bathroom's style.

STANDING CABINETS AND STORAGE TOWERS The range of available self-standing storage is every bit as varied as anything you can put on the wall.

- Buy a standing cabinet with glass fronts, or a storage tower with exposed shelves, if what you want to store is visually appealing.

- If you need a place for bottles of rubbing alcohol and other first-aid supplies, buy a unit with enclosed compartments or frosted-glass doors.

ABOVE LEFT Where space is not an issue in a bathroom, a freestanding cabinet can give you the extra storage you need exactly where you want it. ABOVE RIGHT A wheeled bathroom trolley can provide some of the most versatile storage you can buy. The bins can be used for everything from hair-care products to extra towels, and the mobility of these units lets you position them right where you want them.

- Choose a tower or cabinet based on the amount of surface space you have—tall and skinny towers are best for a bathroom with cramped floor space. Short, broad cabinets are more effective in larger bathrooms.

- Choose a material based on your decorative style. You can select wood cabinets for a traditional look, or go for a sleeker look with a metal-and-glass tower.

- Bathrooms used by a lot of children may call for more durable furniture, such as plastic towers or cabinets. If you want to include a tower in a busy bathroom, pick a pyramid style, which is less likely to tip over. Always make sure any standing cabinet or storage tower is safely secured to the wall.

DOOR BACK In the search for extra storage in the bathroom, the door back has become every bit as viable as a wall. Manufacturers offer hanging towel racks and hooks, over-the-door shelves, and small cabinets. As long as an organizer doesn't interfere with door swing, you can consider it for extra storage.

In cramped quarters, the back of the bathroom door can provide a great place to hang towels. A special over-the-door hook set serves the purpose nicely.

HAMPERS The bathroom is a convenient location for a clothes hamper, which in turn helps keep dirty clothes off the bathroom floor. Hampers range from steel-tube frames with hanging fabric bags to wicker baskets with canvas liners. If space is a concern, you can always hang a laundry bag on the back of a door with a hook. If space is not an issue, you can keep dirty clothes organized and ready to go right into the wash by using a three-compartment hamper with individual bags for whites, bright colors, and darks.

Maintaining Clutter-Free Bathrooms

Even though the bathroom is one of the most used spaces in the house, it requires minimal organization maintenance to keep the room free of clutter. Make maintenance a part of your regular cleaning.

1 Date check

Every 6 months, go through the medicine cabinet and discard medications—both prescription and over-the-counter—that are past their expiration date.

2 Prune publications

Every time you clean the bathroom, take a minute to look through the magazine rack and remove old issues.

3 Inventory assessment

On a monthly basis, check the levels of shampoo, conditioner, bath salts, and other products in the bathroom to see what needs to be replaced. Also check the number of toilet paper rolls you have in stock.

Family and Living Rooms

ZONES

Traditionally, the family room was the informal center of relaxation and recreation for the family, while the living room served as the formal setting for entertaining and socializing. These days the roles usually blend between the two rooms. Many modern and contemporary homes simply don't have both rooms, or one may have been put to another use, such as a home office. Even if your home has two distinct rooms, they are probably both used for living, relaxing, socializing, and entertaining.

Whether two rooms or one, the space presents complex organizational challenges. These rooms fulfill multiple roles, from home theater to party place to family conference center. Each of these roles calls for different types of organization and clutter-busting strategies, especially if you want a permanently clutter-free space.

You'll start with the zone that sees the most use and then proceed to less frequently used areas. Begin where movies and TV are watched, working your way out to peripheral areas of relaxation. As you go along, you'll incorporate solutions to the clutter created by the different functions of the room, including relaxing, socializing, and entertaining.

OPPOSITE A sleek living room incorporates an ottoman as a coffee table. Every piece of furniture has a purpose, and as a result, the room is virtually clutter-free.

ZONE 1

Electronics ● 1 HOUR

Chances are your electronics are the heart of your family or living room. The collection of media and equipment—whether grand or modest—is usually anchored by the TV. But in today's world, you likely have an increasing number of peripheral devices that work with the TV, including the cable or satellite box, a DVD or BluRay player, a video game system, a speaker system, and the family's computer.

Add to all these devices the cords, cables, and bits and pieces that naturally go with them—chargers, remote controls, video games—and the potential for massive clutter is obvious. Bringing order to this often chaotic area will go a long way toward keeping the whole room tidy, and it will make watching TV and listening to music much more enjoyable.

Start by looking at the equipment and media you own now, and think about what you are likely to add in the short term. Then it's just a matter of measuring and matching to find the furniture and solutions to contain your entertainment gear and keep the room neat and comfortable.

ENTERTAINMENT CENTER A key piece of furniture for organizing electronic media, an entertainment center must adequately meet your needs if it is to prevent clutter. The right entertainment center can range from a modest television stand to a wall-filling, adjustable shelf system with custom conduits for cords and wires.

- The first step in finding the right entertainment center is to measure your electronics—depth, width, and height.

- Next, figure out what you want to store in the media center. This should give you a good sense of how much and what type of storage space you need, leading you to the right choice of entertainment center.

This streamlined entertainment center features a large-screen TV and multiple speakers, yet takes up little space and has drawers to hide accoutrements.

The placement of a flat-screen television above the fireplace has become a quickly accepted practice—and with good reason. It places the screen in a convenient viewing position and makes efficient use of blank wall space, eliminating the need for additional special cabinetry.

Adapted centers can be almost any large standing cabinet or shelf unit—from an old armoire to an unused dining-room hutch—that is not specifically designed as an entertainment center. The main requirement is that the piece be deep enough to center your TV, with a shelf or support strong enough to hold the weight. Adapted entertainment centers should:

- Comfortably hold the electronics that work with the TV.

- Have an attached back that allows for holes through which cords can be run.

- Permit proper component spacing and air circulation to cool the equipment.

- Provide room either inside the unit or someplace on the outside for hanging storage if you're storing a music or video collection of traditional CDs, DVDs, and cassette tapes.

Store-bought stands and racks are excellent choices if you simply want a place to put your TV and cable box.

- Stands and racks are sold by the size of the TV, and are available with fixed legs or casters.

- They come tall or wide, in a selection of design styles.

- If you are choosing a TV stand, you'll also want to look at containers for storing DVDs, videos, and CDs, if you have them.

- Don't put a TV on a wall-mounted shelf. Not only are regular cathode-ray TVs too heavy for shelves, they have an off-center balance that makes them prone to tipping when they are not properly supported. Flat-screen TVs are also prone to tipping, but they can be mounted to the wall with special hardware.

VIDEO GAME SYSTEMS Most video game consoles also function as DVD players, and low prices make them attractive even if you use them only for that purpose.

- Depending on your TV, you may need to run the cables from the game box through an RF modulator (a device that makes the signal playable on the TV). This unit is only about the size of a paperback book, but you need to make space for it.

- You'll also need to find a place for the video games themselves. Some look like DVDs and can be stored with CDs or DVDs. Others have different shapes. Manufacturers offer special cases and containers for these games, but it's often cheaper and easier to just set aside a portion of shelf space or drawer space near the game unit for them.

- The controllers require their own storage. If you have enough space in the entertainment center, they can simply be slid in alongside the game console. If space is tight, buy brackets to hold the controllers on the side or front of the entertainment center.

VINYL RECORDS AND OLDER MEDIA Although most of us now listen to music on digital files, some people want to hang on to their traditional stero systems, including CDs, cassette tapes, and even vinyl records.

- Keep your cassettes in special cassette organizers, or stack them on narrow ledge shelves. Deep shelves provide too much space, and the cassettes can become a loose jumble.

- Don't store vinyl records near heat sources.

- Don't stack vinyl records; stand them on edge.

- The best place for vinyl records is a cabinet with a door that will keep the records away from dust, dirt, and moisture.

- If your record collection is too much of a hassle, convert your records to CDs, which are much easier to store.

Entertaining Area 30 MINUTES

Your entertaining area can bring movies or music to life, but you need a comfortable place to watch or listen. This space is defined by the couch, coffee table, and surrounding chairs. The couch itself is rarely a clutter problem. Just keep throw pillows to a minimum—use only those that make you more comfortable. Groups of decorative pillows can too easily become a hiding place for remotes and other small items.

The heart of the entertaining area is the coffee table. It's the natural location for beverages and food, and serves as a parking place for books and magazines. A coffee table is indispensable for keeping things off the floor, and is useful for short-term or specialized storage.

A simple wood trunk can make a great coffee table. The roomy interior offers plenty of long-term storage, and the shape provides stability to ensure that items like flower vases don't fall over when the table is bumped.

COFFEE TABLE Given its role as a centerpiece, choosing the right coffee table is essential to keeping the room organized.

- The first consideration in choosing a coffee table is style. With a little investigation, you can find a piece that seamlessly integrates into your décor and still gives you the storage and organization space you need.

- The ideal coffee table provides enough surface space for beverages and food for the number of people who can fit in the entertaining area.

- Your coffee table should supply enough additional storage for everyday items such as magazines and coasters. In most cases, a shelf below the top is all the extra storage you'll need.

A rattan chest serves as a coffee table in this entertainment lounge, holding seasonal linens and throw pillow covers. The TV is concealed in a pine wardrobe. A side table is clustered with collections of photos so that nothing else can be stored on it.

- The coffee table can also provide drawers for items such as videotapes or the linens you use with a foldout sofa bed.

- If your needs are modest and you just want a place to put the remote and snacks, choose from traditional coffee tables. If your storage needs are more complicated, shop for nontraditional types.

Traditional coffee tables have fixed legs, a simple top, and a shelf or drawers underneath. Crafted of glass, wood, stone, or composite materials, these are meant only to provide a temporary resting place for food and drinks and basic items. The shelf or drawers add longer-term storage.

Nontraditional coffee tables include cube-shaped boxes with lids, chests or trunks, multitier units on casters, and other unusual versions. Most types of unconventional coffee tables can function as mini-closets to store seasonal throws, board games, photo albums, or other items for which there is not enough shelf or closet space. One of the handiest types is an ottoman with a lid and hollow interior. When not being used with a chair, the ottoman can serve as a space-saving coffee table with significant storage under the lid.

STORAGE IN STYLE

Control Remotes: To corral all your remote controls, use your own containers, such as decorative pottery bowls or a nice tray, or choose from the many storage options in stores. Manufacturers provide a plethora of custom solutions, like fancy carousels, simple plastic boxes with multiple cavities, elegant boxes with separate compartments for different remotes, and attractive wood caddies with space for remotes and TV listing guides.

Family rooms and living rooms are made richer with a specific space designed for reading. The couch can certainly serve this purpose, but a reading chair with a good reading light and small side table create a more intimate and suitable space. Set another chair across from the reading chair and the area can also function as an inviting conversational nook for parties or a place for couples to discuss the day's events. The clutter-busting requirement for this area is that the table be minimal—just enough room for a beverage and a book.

A reading area can be kept free of clutter by limiting the amount of space available to set down items.

Shelves   ⏱ 1 HOUR

Although shelves in a living room or family room are commonly devoted to books, they represent flexible storage options for things that don't fit in the entertainment center or other locations in the room. To make the most of the storage, shelf placement needs to be well thought out.

With a ladder for access to the top shelves, this contemporary wall system can reach the ceiling, while an innovative system of sliding panels hide selected sections from view.

- Obviously, shelves can be placed only where they will fit, but they should also be situated as close as possible to where they will be used. For example, a bookshelf will ideally be placed close to a reading chair and reading lamp.
- Available space and storage needs are the key determinants in what type of family- or living-room shelving you use.

Wall-mounted shelves fit in odd spaces, such as over sofas or above wainscoting. They are especially handy for keeping breakables, such as a collection of glass vases or figurines, out of the reach of young children or away from the general traffic flow.

- Don't use wall-mounted shelves for heavy objects, such as a row of coffee-table books or a collection of pottery; the chances of the shelf falling are just too great.
- Wall-mounted shelves with bookends or clamp-on edge stops are great alternatives to CD or DVD holders.

Stand-alone shelves provide more substantial support and far more storage space than wall-mounted units. You can choose an enclosed shelving unit that has a box frame and back piece, shelves with an outside frame but no backing, and shelves supported by a base and vertical braces.

- Where you need enclosed or hidden storage, pick shelving units that incorporate cabinets.

STORAGE IN STYLE

Literary Divisions: Sturdy, freestanding bookshelves supply a lot of storage space, but they can also serve as room dividers. This is especially helpful in a large, long room. Even box-frame bookshelves with back pieces can work: Simply attach two units back to back to create a substantial divider with a wealth of storage.

Wall shelves don't have to be boring to effectively organize books and other items. These contemporary "ladder" shelves are stylish.

- If the floor or wall space where you want to locate the shelves is oddly sized, use tension-pole shelving systems. These use tension-pole supports that collapse or expand to fit varying distances between floor and ceiling. They are equipped with adjustable brackets. The shelves themselves are sold in different widths and depths, so you can decide how wide a given column of shelves will be and how many columns you'll use. The shelf positions in these systems are completely movable.

- If you're comfortable with a more permanent solution, you can have custom bookshelves built to your specifications.

- Always organize books with the largest on the bottom shelves, and smallest on top. This keeps the shelf from tipping and is pleasing to the eye.

- To optimize shelf space, stack same-size books vertically. They take up less shelf space than the same books aligned horizontally.

- Review your collection of books every 6 months or so to make sure you aren't dedicating space on your shelves to books you won't read and don't need.

THE SHELF RULES

1. HAVE A PURPOSE. Individual items must have a reason for being on the shelf. A picture is there to be displayed. Your eyeglasses shouldn't be there, nor should a pile of mail.

2. COLLECT TO DECLUTTER. Collect to declutter. Individual items that are part of a collection, such as figurines or a trio of decorative vases, should be grouped together in their own section of shelf. Alone they can become a part of shelf clutter.

3. CONTAIN WHEN POSSIBLE. Some items you might like to put on a shelf are best kept within a box or other container. Rather than stack a group of votives loose, for example, put them in a decorative wire basket or a handsome box at the end of a row of books.

Fireplace and Mantel 15 MINUTES

The fireplace area—comprising the fireplace and mantel—can be a casual resting place for a lot of what makes its way into living and family rooms. Clutter invites clutter, so this is an area you want to keep as spartan as possible.

FIREPLACE If you have a gas fireplace, you don't need to worry about cleaning ashes or storing firewood. However, wood-burning fireplaces require certain rules.

- The brick or stone footing around the base of the fireplace should be used only for the fireplace accessories and perhaps a decorative urn or sculpture.

- Fireplace tools should be kept organized in a stand or on separate hangers.

- Keep wood tidy in a large, fireproof wood basket, tin bucket, metal cradle, or canvas satchel.

- Keep on hand only the wood you need for a single fire; too much wood means extra mess.

MANTEL Keep the mantel as clear as possible.

- Use it as a showcase for one or two of your favorite decorative (fireproof) pieces. Put a cherished ceramic bowl in the center of the mantel, or place candles in heirloom candleholders at either end.

- The mantel is also a place for items relating to the function of the fireplace, such as a decorative match holder or fire igniter.

- Keep the mantel spare, and people are less likely to absentmindedly place their eyeglasses or a cell phone there. The less there is on the mantel, the more items that don't belong will stick out.

By this point, you've got most of your living and family room in order. Now you need to determine what additional storage you need, and what other types of specialized furniture you want, to complement the socializing, entertaining, or relaxing you do. Additional storage will probably be in the form of concealed space, in furniture such as chests or tables. These not only help with the storage in the living and family rooms, but can also provide long-term storage space for other rooms.

CHESTS A chest provides long-term storage and a place to sit, or a surface for decorative items or lighting. This can substitute for a linen closet, or serve as a handy location for seldom-used board games. A family-room chest is also a good place to display pictures, awards, or mementos of special occasions. The downside to using chests and trunks is their bulk and difficult access. They take up a lot of floor space, can block traffic flow, and are awkward to open and close. Use the top surface for storage or a collection of unbreakable decorative items, to ensure that it doesn't become another clutter-collecting space.

DOLLAR SMART

Booked Up: Stack oversize coffee-table books you've already read to make a nifty table for a reading light or remote-control holder. Use enough books for the height you want and you'll have a stable literary table to complement any décor!

TABLES Side tables and end tables are useful additions to the family and living rooms for both the surface and drawer or shelf space they provide. They can be strategically located to hold lamps where you need light the most—near chairs and other seating. They are also useful for holding small items, such as telephones.

BARS If your entertaining includes drinks, it's a good idea to keep a small bar trolley or caddy in the living or family room. Depending on how much wine, alcohol, and stemware you keep on hand, you can choose from many options, ranging from a simple two-shelf cart to a more elaborate stand-alone bar with pullout doors and compartments. Look for a unit that can fit neatly in a corner when not in use. If you have children in the house, play it safe and buy bar furniture that lets you lock up the alcohol.

A small, portable bar trolley keeps your beverages, glassware, and accessories organized, and fits neatly in a corner.

Windowsills, Pianos, and Other Flat Surfaces

30 MINUTES

The many small, flat surfaces in a home seem to attract clutter like no place else. These surfaces are inviting "temporary" resting places for everything from car keys to spare change. There are two basic strategies for keeping these surfaces clear of clutter.

- The first is the "no-vacancy" rule. This means keeping the surfaces bare at all times—anything that doesn't belong should be immediately removed.

- A more appropriate strategy for busy homes is to create a focal point. Use the flat surface as a showcase area, with one central display. For example, use your most beautiful vase full of dried flowers as the center of attention atop an upright piano. By creating a focal point, anything else put on the surface sticks out.

Maintaining Clutter-Free Family Rooms and Living Rooms

The varied zones in living and family rooms call for a simple, clutter-busting maintenance strategy that can work across the space.

1 Two for one
Integrate your "clutter check" as part of the regular dusting and vacuuming in the room. Return anything out of place to its proper location, especially if the location is in another room.

2 Periodical update
Once a month, check the magazines and catalogs on your coffee table, and recycle those that are out of date.

3 Disc order
Every few months, make sure that your video games and DVDs aren't piling up. If you need more storage space, buy an extra media tower or rack.

CHAPTER 5

Dining Rooms

ZONES

1 Dining Table
2 Hutch or China Cabinet
3 Sideboard
4 Additional Storage

The dining room is one of the simpler rooms to organize. That's because it's focused on one purpose: meals. You might use the dining room for casual dining from time to time, but for the most part, the room is used for special occasions. This well-defined purpose leaves you with a clear goal in organizing: to make serving and enjoying meals as pleasant and simple as possible.

Your dining room may not necessarily be a separate room. In some homes, it's open floor space next to the kitchen, or set at the end of a long living room. Whether a room in its own right or a space you carve out, the dining room is defined by the furniture you use there and the "service circle."

The service circle incorporates the dining table and the area around it. The service circle may also include some sort of storage cabinet—from a simple hutch to a more ornate china cabinet—for crystal, china, and silver. If you have the floor space, the dining room should include a sideboard or side table that provides additional storage underneath and a place on top to put food that won't fit or will get in the way on the table.

Organize this room starting with the table. In each zone, remove everything that is currently stored there, and determine which items have something to do with serving, presenting, eating, or enjoying a meal. Those items that don't should be moved to another, more appropriate part of the house, or should be given away. Once you've decided what needs to be stored in each zone, you'll know how much and what type of storage is required to completely organize the dining room.

OPPOSITE Even a small dining room can be kept clutter-free by storing table linens, china, and glassware in a tall corner cabinet.

Elegance is the hall-
mark of this simple,
functional, and well-
organized dining room.

1

A sturdy sideboard is
the focal point in this
dining room. It offers
a wide top surface for
serving platters when
needed, and a great
deal of large and small
storage options in the
form of cabinets and
drawers.

2

A stylish hutch provides ample shelf space for signature pieces that deserve prominence. Note how a vase has been placed on top to ensure that the surface doesn't become the resting place for clutter.

3

The table has been laid for tea, with a graceful runner and tea set. The setting is pleasing to the eye and can be left on the table until the next meal, discouraging anyone from setting other items on the table.

The dining room table is for eating, drinking, and socializing after meals. Activities other than dining—such as homework and bill-paying—can scratch a table's surface and often leave behind clutter. As noted in the box below, reinforce the singular purpose of this room by keeping the table set (see photo opposite). The idea is to dissuade anyone from using the table for anything other than dining.

The central storage issue concerning the dining-room table is what to do with the leaves and pads, if any (obviously not an issue if you have a glass dining-room table). A closet near the dining room—especially a closet that doesn't see much use—is the ideal location for removable table leaves. Wherever you put them, make sure they won't get scratched, experience extremes of heat or cold, or be exposed to water. If your dining room is spacious, consider keeping your extra table leaves in the table.

HIDE A LEAF If you're considering a new dining-room table and need one that can adapt to larger and smaller groups, shop for one with self-storing leaves. The most common are those with "butterfly" leaves that simply fold in and slide under the surface of the table. Self-storing leaves eliminate the need to find a safe place to put them, and they are easier to use.

INSIDE SCOOP

Space Shuffle: Not every homeowner is fortunate enough to have an eat-in kitchen; sometimes the dining-room table is the site of every meal. In this case, leave the table set so that people are deterred from leaving clutter on the table between meals.

This round table in a cozy dining room includes place settings that discourage clutter and add an element of elegance to the room.

The traditional hutch or china cabinet is both showcase and storage. It's a place to put signature or heirloom pieces on display, and one to hide dining-room essentials, such as linens, serving trays, and sterling silverware. Hutches and cabinets come in many different sizes and shapes, but the purpose is the same: to organize all the things you'll use for eating and drinking. Because most of what you store in a hutch has both sentimental and real-dollar value, leave plenty of room around individual items to protect against breakage. As with other rooms and zones in the house, a key principle in organizing the hutch or china cabinet is to store items by type.

Plate racks are a handy way to store your favorite dishes, and this simple hutch includes them, plus hanging pegs, cabinet space, and a serving area.

CHINA Fine china is durable enough to withstand decades of use, but delicate enough for improper storage to cause chipping or scratching. The three basic ways to store china are stacking, racking, and packing. How you store yours depends on the type of space you have and whether you want to display the china.

Stack china where it is unlikely to receive any kind of blow to the edges of plates and saucers or lips of cups. Place buffer sheets between stacked plates to protect them from scratching one another. Buffers can be felt pads, cardboard squares, or even thick cloth napkins. Never stack china cups. Line them up in rows.

Racks for plates and dishes make efficient use of storage space. These are simple wood or plastic frames with slots that hold plates apart from one another and prevent scratching and chipping. They are made to sit securely on cabinet shelves and organize plates so that you can easily remove them as needed. Use softwood shelf racks that can accommodate your entire set of plates and saucers. Choose a rack with a shelf for rows of china cups, so all your china can be kept together.

Pack away china when there is not enough room for it in display storage, or if you use it infrequently and want to ensure against breakage. Inexpensive, quilted china-packing cases come in all shapes and sizes to accommodate the number and size of pieces in your collection. These have zippered openings to keep dust and dirt away from your china while it is in storage. Keep the packed china in the cabinet area of your hutch.

CRYSTAL The surface of fine crystal is softer and more prone to scratching than regular glass.

- Leave plenty of room around your crystal pieces, whether they are small cordial glasses or large vases.

- Never store something inside a piece of crystal.

- Crystal stemware is most fragile along the stem, so don't hang these glasses from stemware racks.

- Since the rim of crystal glassware is fragile, store glasses standing upright, with plenty of room around them to prevent breakage.

- Avoid keeping crystal on or under adjustable shelves; any jostling of the shelf can cause expensive breakage.

- You can also store crystal in padded boxes or containers, such as the ones used for china.

SILVER Sterling silver is extremely sensitive to its environment. To protect your silverware and serving pieces from tarnish and corrosion, store them correctly. First and foremost, keep silver pieces out of circulating air.

- Store your silver away from other metals, in a silverware chest or box. These are made with tarnish-resistant liners and cavities for the different pieces in your set.

- You can also put the silver in tarnish-resistant storage bags, but keep the bags out of the sun and away from moisture.

- It's usually best to keep the silverware in its container in a hutch cabinet or drawer. But many silverware boxes are relatively airtight and are crafted of attractive hardwoods, so you may want to keep the box on a shelf or on top of the sideboard.

THE INSIDE SCOOP

Corner Store: If space is tight in your dining room, consider using a corner hutch or hutches. These triangular cabinets nestle into the corner of the room and are an efficient use of space and a way to keep valuables out of the flow of traffic in the room. Two of these placed in adjacent corners can provide about the same amount of storage as a standard-sized hutch.

THE INSIDE SCOOP

Herb Help: Protect your linens and keep them smelling lovely with a little help from the garden. Dried lavender sprigs in the folds of your dining-room linens will repel insects and lightly perfume the fabric.

LINENS You can certainly store your special-occasion tablecloths and fine napkins in a linen closet or wherever you put your beddings, but in keeping with the idea of storing items near where they're used, it's best to stow dining-room linens in the dining room.

- Place linens in a concealed area of the hutch (or the sideboard, if you don't have room in the hutch), and keep cedar blocks with the linens to repel insects.

- Don't place fine linens directly on a wood shelf, because the wood and its finish may contain acids that can discolor the cloth over time. Use a shelf liner or keep your linens in a box.

- Heirloom lace and embroidered tablecloths should be wrapped in acid-free paper for maximum protection. Find the paper in art supply or fabric stores.

- Regularly rotate and refold your linens to prevent creases from becoming permanent.

The role of the sideboard is to hold food while serving, and to store vessels and utensils used in serving food. The ideal dining-room sideboard includes an uncluttered top surface and ample storage below in the form of shelves or cabinets.

TABLETOP The top surface of a sideboard provides a place to put large serving dishes from the kitchen that wouldn't otherwise fit on the dining-room table during meals. It's also a place to work with the food you are serving, such as the cutting of a large sheet cake, which would be difficult on the dining table itself. In between meals, the top serves as a location for those special items you don't want to keep on the table, such as a candelabrum and cream-and-sugar sets. The common thread that all these items share is utility. If it isn't used for a meal, it doesn't belong on the sideboard.

LOWER STORAGE The shelves or cabinets underneath the sideboard's top should be dedicated to oversized serving items, including punch bowls, large decorative serving trays, serving bowls, and special oversized pitchers. This can also be a great place to store linens, but don't place them touching other items or the wood shelf or they may become stained.

The collection of family photos on this sideboard serves a dual purpose: It provides a beautiful display, and it keeps clutter at bay.

Additional Storage ⏱ 30 MINUTES

Depending on the size and capacity of your hutch and sideboard, you may need to find extra storage space for small seasonal items, replacement supplies, and other items that just don't fit in those zones. Because there is rarely enough room around a table—given the space needed to comfortably pull chairs in and out—more furniture is usually not the answer. Instead, turn to wall space for additional dining-room storage.

Shelves can provide attractive, much-needed storage positioned out of traffic flow.

- Use shelves to store decorative boxes containing supplies like festive special-occasion napkin rings or as display storage for collections such as demitasse cups.

- Use them to hold seasonal centerpieces or candleholders that don't fit on top of the sideboard.

- Special ledge shelves with thin, routed channels are excellent for storing and displaying sets of three or four plates, or larger ceramic serving dishes.

Hanging plate racks are a way to store your special serving dishes or dessert plates while creating decorative interest on the wall. You can select from wrought-iron types that provide a frame for the plates, more discreet wire hangers that let the plate "float" on the wall, or simple wood types. Just make sure you hang the plates where they won't get bumped.

Wine racks are a natural addition to the dining room, placing the bottles where they are most likely to be opened and served. Position your wine rack out of direct sunlight and away from any heat sources. Always store bottles on their side so the corks stay moist and prevent oxygen from reaching the wine. The average temperature range in a home is not optimal for wine, but won't cause any noticeable deterioration over a period of a few months. If you're looking to store wine longer, consider the basement (see pages 170 and 171) or use a wine refrigerator.

Maintaining Clutter-Free Dining Rooms

The dining room is generally out of the traffic flow of the house, making it one of the easier rooms to keep free of clutter. Maintenance is still important, however.

1 Dining-room beat

Every few days, walk through the dining room and do a clutter inspection to ensure that nobody has left items on the dining-room table or sideboard. Remove whatever you find, placing it back where it belongs.

2 The forbidden zone

If your family is in the habit of using the dining-room table as a place to store homework, dry cleaning, and mail, make a small sign reminding them that this area is off limits.

ZONES

1 Basement Emergency Area
2 Basement Workshop
3 Basement Hazardous Material Storage
4 Basement Food and Beverage Storage
5 Basement General Shelving and Cabinets
6 Attic Clothing Storage
7 Attic Memorabilia Space
8 Attic Holiday Decorations
9 Attic General Storage

Even though the basement and attic are two distinct rooms, they are grouped together here because they share a central purpose: to provide long- and short-term storage for other areas of the house. The other reason to consider the two in one section is because many houses don't have both. That's why you should approach the zones in this chapter according to your home's layout and your individual needs. Choose the zones that apply to you and organize them in an order that makes sense for your circumstances.

As alike as these areas may be, the location of the zones takes into account the fundamental differences between basements and attics. Basements are generally easier to access, so supplies such as beverages and food bought in bulk are more logically stored there. But basements are also damp, so anything prone to mold and mildew, such as clothing, finds a more fitting home in the attic.

Whether you have an attic, basement, or both, the first step toward organizing the space is removing everything that is currently there and doing a thorough cleaning. As unpleasant as this may sound, it's essential because these rooms are prone to insect and rodent infestation. If you have pest problems, you need to deal with them before organizing the space, or you'll just wind up making a mess of your newly clutter-free room once you're forced to deal with the issue.

Clearing everything out also gives you the chance to winnow out boxes and belongings that you no longer need or want. Donate or discard these items.

OPPOSITE While most attics are dark and used for storage, this previously unused space was turned into an attractive mini study. The window offers natural light, and the small desk and chairs fit easily under the slanted ceiling.

The general rule of assigning specific locations to each type of item you store applies to the basement and attic more than any other room in the house.

In some instances, you'll have to transfer a given zone to a different room. For example, if you have children, hazardous materials must be stored under lock and key. But those products normally stored in a basement can go into a locked garage cabinet if your home doesn't have a basement.

Although you should clean out the basement in one session, don't try to organize the whole space at once—there's simply too great a chance that you'll fall behind and will have to start over. When you're organizing the various zones, don't get overly ambitious; take them one at a time. The times assigned to each zone are fairly standard, regardless of how big or small your basement or attic might be, but the times can be considerable, as you'll see.

These zone guidelines don't apply to converted attics or basements. If you have turned a dry basement into an extra bedroom or a child's playroom, or finished the attic for use as a home office, consult the appropriate chapter for organization strategies that relate to those rooms.

THE INSIDE SCOOP

Pet Pests: Never store open bags of pet food or other edibles, such as birdseed, in the attic or basement. The food will attract rodents and insects. If you must store edibles in one of these rooms, transfer them from their original packaging into tightly sealed plastic containers.

STORAGE IN STYLE

Color Guard: Create a quick-identification system and an attractive look for your basement or attic by color-coding what you store. For example, place holiday decorations in red boxes, clothes in blue, and so on.

This basement storage space has been configured with shelves and drawers to accommodate a wide range of belongings.

Basement Emergency Area

Homeowners in today's world must be prepared for natural and man-made disasters. The first step is to create a home emergency kit and store it in the basement, where you and your family should gather in the event of an emergency. (If you don't have a basement, keep the kit in a room with few windows and other openings; you should be able to block the few you have with duct tape and plastic sheeting.) The U.S. Department of Homeland Security (www.dhs.gov) recommends that homeowners keep a 3-day supply of food and water on hand for each member of the household. The government specifically recommends the following items.

WATER At least 3 gallons of water per person, sealed in plastic jugs.

FOOD An adequate supply of canned and dried food for each person, for at least 3 days.

CLOTHES One change of clothes for each person in the house.

SUPPLIES These should include a flashlight, a battery-powered radio, extra batteries, a complete first-aid kit, toilet articles, backup prescription medicines, a can opener, and duct tape and heavy-duty garbage bags to seal windows and doors. You should also include a wrench (to turn off utilities), dust masks, and moist hand and face wipes.

Store the emergency supplies in a clearly designated, accessible area. Keep all the supplies for the kit in bags in sealed plastic tubs, and mark them with the label "Emergency Kit." Include a list of emergency contacts in the kit.

The keys to getting the most out of your home workshop are a physical setup that lets you work smoothly without creating clutter, and safety elements that ensure your projects present no danger to you or your family.

WORKTABLE The two major requirements of a good worktable are that it provides adequate space—so your supplies and equipment aren't cramped—and that it be sturdy. You can choose from wood, metal, or plastic tables, but wood is often the best choice. Wood tables are usually forgiving of spills and other accidents, and it's fairly easy to make a crude wood table to fit your needs with just a little plywood and 4 two-by-fours.

This basement workshop is kept in order with locking cabinets, tool drawers, and an integrated work surface. Outdoor-use tools are hung on the walls, freeing up space in the garage.

SHELVES AND CABINETS Most basement work areas benefit from the addition of shelves or cabinets.

- Metal shelves are the best choice for work areas because they are durable, generally lightweight, nonabsorbent (making them easy to clean), and easy to install.

- Cabinets are perfect for storing chemicals and other supplies or equipment that could pose a health risk. If you have children in the house, keep the cabinet locked.

- Depending on the space you have, use a standing cabinet or one mounted on the wall or near to the worktable.

- Whether you are using shelves, a cabinet, or both, supplies and equipment should be separated and organized by type to make it easy to find what you need when you need it.

TOOL STORAGE Tools and their accessories, such as drill bits, must be conveniently organized to avoid clutter and to keep them from getting lost. Some tool sets come with stand-alone racks that keep all of these items in order. If the tools for your handiwork don't have their own rack, you'll need to create or buy a holder for them. Choose from "hobby" cases that are great for small items, such as supplies for tying fishing flies; basic toolboxes; wall-mounted, magnetic tool-holders; or stepped benchtop organizers.

As part of organizing your work area, you'll need to include safety features, where necessary, to make your projects risk free.

STORAGE IN STYLE

Tool's Gold: A handyman's tool belt is remarkably versatile for holding many different types of work-shop tools. Hang one across the front of your workbench to keep tools close at hand or carefully suspend the belt overhead from the rafters.

VENTILATION Many home hobbies involve unhealthy fumes that should be ventilated from the confined space of the basement. Proper ventilation requires both a source for fresh air and a fan to vent fumes. Look for basic ventilation systems—usually consisting of an exhaust fan, ductwork (such as flexible tubing), and a hood. These can be found at large home centers or home-heating companies. Select one with the proper CFM (cubic feet per minute) rating and hood design for the size of your space.

FIRE SAFETY Many projects, including stained-glass crafting and wood etching, require working with an open flame or flammable materials. If your work involves fire dangers, mount the appropriate fire extinguisher in clear view as close as possible to the work area. Keep the route to the fire extinguisher, and to basement exits, clear at all times. Familiarize yourself with the instructions: During a fire is the worst time to learn how to use an extinguisher.

WASTE DISPOSAL Most chemicals used in home-based workshops should not be dumped down your drain. Keep these substances in appropriate containers and take them to your local hazardous waste disposal center (contact your sanitation department for guidelines and locations).

THE INSIDE SCOOP

Flame Killers: Whether protecting against flammable hobby materials or common household accidents, such as grease fires, it's wise to keep the right fire extinguisher in close proximity to areas that present fire dangers. Extinguishers are rated for the types of fires they fight: "Class A" for common combustibles such as cloth, wood, and paper; "Class B" for fires caused by flammable liquids such as gasoline or grease; and "Class C" for electrical fires. ("Class D" are special extinguishers for use on flammable metals and are not usually used in the home.) Multiclass extinguishers—rated "ABC"—are the preferred choice for the home because they extinguish the widest range of fires.

Basement Hazardous Material Storage

 30 MINUTES

Hazardous materials include cleaning supplies that could be dangerous to small children and pets, flammable materials such as paint thinner, and pesticides. In households with children, these products should be kept in a locked cabinet, clearly marked with the contents and a "DANGER" label.

- A metal cabinet is better than a wood unit because metal won't soak up spills and isn't flammable.

- Position the cabinet out of the general traffic flow in the basement. Clearly mark the cabinet so that any emergency personnel responding to a fire will quickly know what's in the cabinet.

This storage area is ideal for storing hazardous materials. It's out of the general traffic flow, and it includes a locked cabinet.

Basement Food and Beverage Storage

Positioned far from work and hazardous material storage areas, the food zone in your basement is a backup to your kitchen, one that lets you take advantage of the significant discounts available in price clubs and provides an alternative to a cluttered pantry. The requirements for this type of storage are that the food and beverage be up off the floor and in an area that is easy to get to, and that the storage support is stable and large enough to handle all your bulk buys. Shelves are the preferred option for storing food, because you can see the inventory you have on hand. Position stored goods in order of weight—canned goods and beverages on the lower shelves, other dry goods and plastics on the upper shelves.

DRY AND CANNED FOODS Follow the pantry rules, plus a few more guidelines.

- Group foods by type in basement storage.

- Be strict about rotating stock. Placing newer purchases in back of old ensures that you use the freshest ingredients and helps you detect and remedy any rodent problems before the damage is excessive.

- Because of the basement's propensity toward high humidity, dry-goods packaging should be nonabsorbent. If you want to store materials that are in absorbent packaging, you'll need to transfer them to plastic bins or tubs with tight-fitting lids to protect against mold.

- Allow for plenty of air circulation around the stored goods.

GENERAL BEVERAGES Keep these tips in mind.

- Whenever possible, keep canned and bottled beverages in their cases. This is neater and allows for easier storage.

- Try to store larger economy-size bottles or jugs in a row, arranged by type of beverage. The aim is to prevent tipping and spills.

- Don't leave open beverage containers in the basement—they are an invitation to pests and are spills waiting to happen.

- If you've bought tall, thin bottles, keep them grouped in a shallow plastic tray or bin. This will not only help prevent spills, it will also contain any that do occur.

- Clean any spills promptly to avoid attracting insects.

- Beverage storage should always be located away from any basement heat sources, such as dryer vents, boilers, hot-water pipes, and so on.

WINE The basement is often the perfect place to store a wine collection. Wine is best kept in relative darkness, at a consistent temperature around 55°F, with humidity around 70 to 80 percent.

- Keep your wine away from basement windows and far from heat sources such as a boiler or hot-water pipes.

- Store the wine by type to make it easy to find the bottle you want.

- Don't keep wine bottles in their original cardboard cases. The material is likely to absorb moisture and weaken over time.

Box racks are a traditional type of wine storage constructed with a wood exterior and crisscrossing interior wood shelves that form diamond- or square-shaped cubbies for the bottles. These look nice and are extremely stable, and

the units can be stacked—a handy feature when you want to expand your wine collection. The only drawback is that it is difficult to see the wine labels without pulling out the bottles. Keep the racks up off the floor, just in case the basement ever floods. Put them on cinder blocks or stack them on a sturdy table.

Shelf racks are more adaptable. These expandable shelving units are freestanding with slots for the bottles. The racks can be stacked row by row to slowly increase storage as needed. Although not as stable as box racks, most shelf-rack designs let you view the labels without pulling out the bottles. Shelf racks are available in wood, metal, and plastic.

Metal racks of any type must be coated with a rust-inhibiting finish if they will be used in the basement.

ZONE 5

Basement General Shelving and Cabinets
30 MINUTES

The basement offers a place to put overflow from the garage or garden shed, and can accommodate odds and ends from the household as well. Shelves are excellent for storing seasonal items, such as plastic plant-pots and hoses, which would not fare well in the winter temperatures of a garage or shed. Be aware that bagged materials, such as potting soil and manure, are prone to leaks. If you keep these materials in the basement, consider transferring them to 5-gallon plastic buckets (the type restaurants use). You can purchase these buckets, with lids, at home centers and nurseries. Hang hoses brought in for the winter from hooks affixed to joists.

Attic Clothing Storage 1 HOUR

As diligent as you might be about weeding out your wardrobe on a regular basis, you will inevitably need to store some clothing. You may want to put away the clothes your first child has outgrown so that a younger sibling can wear them in the future. Or you may want to keep favorite outfits from when your child was very young. Depending on what part of the country you live in, you'll likely need to rotate seasonal clothing in and out of storage. Whatever the situation, an attic can prove invaluable for keeping clothes in good shape over a long period of time. Whether storing clothing on hangers or in boxes, make sure the articles are completely clean before putting them away; even a little dirt can create bad odors and stains, and can attract insects over time.

FOLDED CLOTHES Follow these tips for successful storage.

- Be sure to fold clothes carefully for long-term storage so you don't damage the garments.

- Use the right size and number of boxes for the clothes you are storing; cramming clothes into a small box will only lead to permanent crease marks and fabric deterioration.

- Look for waterproof, vented plastic boxes for clothes other than wool garments. Store wool pieces in cedar chests, with lids that seal tightly.

- Protect clothes in plastic or cardboard boxes against insect damage by putting in mothballs, cedar blocks, or lavender sachets. Make sure the boxes are sealed well, or the insect repellents won't work.

- As an extra precaution, include a drying agent such as silica gel, which will absorb moisture and prevent mold and mildew from ruining clothes.

A handy portable closet is essential for attic clothing storage. This one features fabric panels that zip shut to protect against dust and dirt, and a shelf over the hanging rods.

- Precious clothes and heirlooms, such as lace tablecloths, should be wrapped in acid-free tissue paper—and the box should be lined with acid-free paper—which you can find in art stores and at many dry cleaners.

- Organize garments within their boxes so that sweaters are grouped with sweaters, children's clothes are grouped by size and article, and so on.

- Make it easy to find the clothes you need by affixing labels to the exteriors of the storage containers, and ensure that the boxes don't migrate to other parts of the attic. Duct tape marked with a permanent ink marker also makes for long-lasting labels.

THE CLOTHES STORAGE RULES

1. REMOVE ACCESSORIES. Jewelry and decorative ornamentation on clothing can cause rips and tears and, depending on the jewelry, can stain other garments. Remove brooches and pins from shirts and jackets before hanging.

2. EMPTY POCKETS. Loose change, keys, or other items stored in pockets of a garment can cause permanent distortion of the fabric.

3. BUTTON UP. Close all fasteners on clothing, including buttons, zippers, and snaps, to help the garment maintain its proper shape.

4. CLEAN FIRST. Dry-clean or wash clothes one last time, rinsing well to ensure that stains are gone and that no lasting traces of scented detergent or bleach—which can damage stored garments—remain. Never starch clothes before storing; it can cause yellowing and attract insects.

5. BAG FREE. Do not store clothing in plastic bags, including the plastic that your dry cleaner uses to protect your garment. Plastic traps moisture and can cause mold and mildew.

The Wheel Thing: For easy access to seasonal clothes you want to store outside the bedroom, consider a rolling closet. The closet will stop when it hits a slanted attic ceiling, presenting the opportunity to position boxed clothes behind the hanging garments in the angled space behind the closet. The best rolling closets have canvas or fabric covers with all-around zippers and cedar floors. If the attic is equipped with a closet, put hanging garments in their own canvas storage bags.

HANGING CLOTHES Some clothes, such as dresses and coats, should be hung to maintain their shape. Vented fabric garment bags with zippers and opaque, insect-resistant linings are ideal for precious clothes that you want to protect as thoroughly as possible.

A simple rolling hanging bar is a quick solution for short-term clothing storage in the attic. A bottom shelf lets you store flat items such as the plastic shoebox shown here.

Attic Memorabilia Space 1 HOUR

Some memorabilia have sentimental and historical value, such as your father's war medals or the samplers your great-grandmother made. Others have monetary value, such as antique statues or stained-glass panels handed down through generations. Some memorabilia have both. Memorabilia stored in your attic may include the personal souvenirs you've collected over time and family heirlooms that, for any number of reasons, you choose not to display. The goal is to protect it all against breakage and deterioration. Lined and padded memory chests are ideal containers for your precious objects. These come in a variety of sizes, with compartments, drawers, pullout bins, and other configurations. Pick the one that best accommodates what you need to store. If you decide to put your memorabilia in plain plastic or cardboard boxes, make sure all breakables are thoroughly protected by padding, and buy opaque boxes that will prevent light from fading the colors in fabrics and painted pieces.

Attic Holiday Decorations 15 MINUTES

Attic storage is ideal for delicate—and not so delicate—holiday decorations. Once largely limited to holiday ornaments and lights, decorations these days may include fake skeletons for Halloween, Thanksgiving centerpieces and candles, and even Fourth of July banners and yard decorations. To make sure your decorations stay in good shape, dedicate a corner of the attic to them.

- If you use decorations for only one or two holidays, just stack them in a column of boxes.

- If you have a bigger collection of holiday decorations, use standing shelves to keep everything in one place.

- Don't store decorations loose. You can find a specialized box or container for just about any type of decoration. For example, wreaths can be put away in protective storage bags or octagonal boxes made just for wreaths.

A durable plastic ornament box can be the best option where the box is likely to see rough treatment and the goal is protecting against breakage.

ORNAMENTS You'll find an amazing diversity of options when it comes to storing Christmas ornaments. You can select from padded cardboard boxes, fancy molded-plastic units, or even wood chests with individual compartments for each ornament. Choose ornament boxes based on how much you're willing to spend and how precious your collection is—wood chests offer the most protection, but cost the most. Plastic is durable and will absorb shocks when the box is moved around, but if there is little traffic in the attic, a cardboard ornament box may provide all the protection you need. The most important element in your choice is buying a container that will store the number of ornaments you have. If your collection expands annually, re-evaluate your storage needs when it comes time to take down the tree.

DECORATIVE LIGHTS Keep your strings of holiday lights tidy with a spooling light-string organizer. If you have several strings, such as outdoor sets and the sets you use on a Christmas tree, you can buy special plastic storage boxes with slots for each organizer and cavities for extra bulbs.

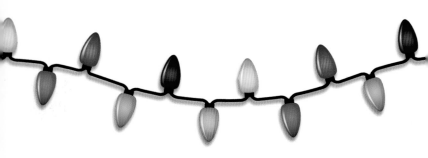

ZONE 9
Attic General Storage

Extra room in the attic can serve as long-term storage for papers
and files that need to be kept for legal or tax reasons. Files should be
kept in file-holder boxes, with built-in supports that keep the files
upright and organized. Label the boxes and stack them neatly in
the most out-of-the-way corner in the attic. Legal documents and
important papers that you want to store in the attic should be kept
in a fireproof or fire-resistant box or safe.

Color-coding makes organizing boxes in the attic a much easier chore.

Maintaining Clutter-Free Basements and Attics

Basements and attics often become the dumping grounds for household goods that have no place else to go. Consequently, you need to be vigilant in these areas. Every 6 months or so, conduct an organizational review of your basement and attic to make sure the zones are still in order.

1 Emergency update

Every 3 months, check your emergency supplies to confirm that batteries are still good, equipment is functioning, and food and water supplies are not leaking or damaged.

2 Seasonal survey

With the change of seasons, check on clothing in long-term storage to ensure that it is still neatly organized, and that no moths or other insects or rodents have gotten to them. Make sure that boxes are still stacked in a logical order.

CHAPTER 7

Garages and Sheds

ZONES

1. Recycling Center
2. Hand Tools
3. Power Tools
4. Yard and Garden Equipment and Supplies
5. Sports Gear
6. Car Care

G̲arages and sheds are traditionally rough, unfinished spaces, exposed to greater variations in temperature and humidity than the house itself. These structures are best suited for storing equipment and supplies that are normally used outside, such as power tools, gardening equipment, outdoor furniture, and sports gear. All the information for zones in this chapter pertains to both sheds and garages.

Organizing a garage or outbuilding is a matter of "sectionalizing." Each type of equipment or product will get a specific section of wall or floor space, clearly separate from other sections. This way, you will easily be able to determine where things go. However, some outdoor structures are so small that they are limited to one type of storage, such as garden tools and supplies. In that case, use the guidelines for that particular zone.

Garages tend to become household catchalls. That's why before you start organizing the zones of the garage you'll need to pull everything out. Get rid of all the things you don't need, and determine what stays in the garage and what should go elsewhere. Once you've created a clean, blank slate to work with, start planning which zones you'll use.

Note that the times listed for these zones assume a full house of active people. You may do much less gardening and fewer outdoor activities; in this case, you can expect to scale back the amount of time each zone will take.

OPPOSITE Garages are versatile spaces that can be set up with many different storage options. Here, gardening tools on Peg-Board share space with equipment on a worktable and shelves.

False Attic: Create a simple, concealed overhead storage space in the garage by laying thin plywood sheets across the overhead joists that span the width of the garage. This gives you additional long-term storage for any overflow from your attic.

Obviously, your garage may not have all the zones listed. But whatever zones you include, lay out a plan for accommodating them in your garage. Using a pad and pencil, or chalk to mark the garage floor, decide which zones go where. Then start organizing, zone by zone.

Garage wall systems are a way to organize the entire garage at once. These systems use standard-ized slotted wall panels that are hung in rows on the garage wall studs (metal studs are installed in the case of masonry walls). You then choose from a range of specially designed benches, cabinets, shelves, and accessories that are constructed to hang from the slots in the wall panels. This gives you the opportunity to customize garage storage to suit your needs.

Recycling Center 30 MINUTES

It's often surprising how messy a few weeks' accumulation of newspapers and recyclable food containers can be. How can you organize this chaos?

- Identify the recycling area in your garage. For most homes, the best area is right next to the door leading into the garage.

- Next, you need to choose appropriate containers. Most municipalities require that you separate recyclables into three categories: paper products, glass and plastics, and metals. Think about how much of these materials you collect between recycling pickup days. Check what your town requires, then pick up appropriate containers that provide enough room for you to even miss one recycling pickup.

- To make things easier, choose different colors for your containers and label them in large letters (unless your municipality already requires that certain colors be used for different recyclables).

- If you're willing to spend the money, you can buy premade recycling centers, with bins that are contained in their own framework. These top-of-the-line structures have lids and include bins that tilt out.

- You can certainly make do with separate bins, as long as they are the right size. For a household with only a few people, you may only need shallow plastic tubs. For a family of four or more, you may need small garbage cans.

Almost every homeowner has experienced the frustration of looking high and low for a particular hand tool needed to complete a home repair job. Small but crucial, hand tools all too easily slip into cracks and crevices, drop behind a worktable, or disappear mysteriously when they don't have their own clearly identified home. That's why organizing your hand tools is a huge step in making your life easier (and in saving money on replacing those that seem to drift away).

HANGING STORAGE Decades ago, home handymen developed an amazingly simple and efficient system for keeping hand tools in order. They put up a sheet of Peg-Board over the garage workbench, and hung tools off Peg-Board hooks. To make things even easier, they traced outlines around the tools so they could quickly see if any tool was missing, what the tool was, and where it should be put back. This system still works wonders. Manufacturers have taken the idea one step further, creating custom perforated panels, with hanging pins specially made to support small tools, and special accessories, such as hanging chisel trays and screwdriver racks. You can also keep tools in special hanging cabinets attached to wall studs, which lets you lock them up. Although they can be expensive, these are great places to store valuable collections of hand tools.

BOX STORAGE Every home should have a basic tool kit, including a set of Phillips-head and standard screwdrivers, a hammer, a tape measure, and other simple hand tools.

- Although you can hang up all of these, home projects are made much easier with a small, portable toolbox. Popular toolboxes come equipped with sturdy handles, and are increasingly made of lightweight but strong plastic construction. Look for one with small utility drawers to hold a modest collection of screws, nails, and washers.

Stage Craft: Borrow an organizational strategy from professional contractors, who use a site "stage." When you tackle a repair project, such as replacing a faucet, lay out all the tools you need on a clean rag before you start. Then put the tools back on the rag as soon as you are through using them. Once you're done with the job, it's easy to transport the tools and put them back where they belong.

This basement workshop is kept in order with ample cabinetry, a Peg-Board for tools, and an integrated work surface. Sports equipment is hung on the wall, freeing up space in the garage.

- If your tool collection is more extensive, you need to consider a larger standing or rolling toolbox. Most of these are metal, and come with a variety of different depth drawers, attached cabinets, and open shelves. Choose the right type based on how many tools you need to store. An added advantage to standing or rolling tool chests is that the top can be an excellent work surface. Select a rolling toolbox for maximum flexibility in placement. The casters lock when the unit has to be stationary.

THE HAND TOOL QUESTIONS

1. Do you centralize your home repair tools at a bench in the garage? If so, Peg-Board tool storage may be the most efficient way to store your tools and keep them ready for use.

2. Do you own a great number and/or diversity of tools, such as car repair and general home repair tools? A large rolling chest can provide a lot of separate compartments for tools of different sizes and shapes. Combine this with a smaller toolbox for frequently used tools like common sizes of screwdrivers, hammers, and pliers.

3. Are your tools extremely valuable? If you have pricey tools, such as vintage woodworking chisels and planes, store them in locked cabinets or boxes.

Power Tools 30 MINUTES

Today, most power tools come with carrying cases, and are often sold in complete sets with extra blades or bits contained in the same case as the power tool. If you have an older power tool without a container, you can buy a carrying case to accommodate the tool and accessories—a great way to keep things organized.

- Store power tools adjacent to the hand-tool zone, because power tools are often used in conjunction with hand tools.

- For safety—and because they are expensive—you may want to store power tools in a closed and locked cabinet if you have children in the household.

- Dedicate different shelves in the cabinet to different types of tools, such as cutting, drilling, shaping, and so on.

- If your power tool has a cord, use heavy-duty twist ties to keep the cord in a tidy loop.

- You can also opt to hang power tools—from their handles or body—on a heavy-duty rack made specifically for this purpose. Never hang a tool from its power cord; you can damage the cord and make the tool unsafe to use.

- If all your power tools are contained in their own cases, you can store them in a row on a sturdy, deep shelf. Position the shelf out of the reach of children.

Special racks for individual power tools can keep them out of the reach of youngsters, and ready for use when you need them.

Yard and Garden Equipment and Supplies

 I HOUR

Even a small yard with a couple of flower beds and borders requires a host of supplies and equipment. Basic lawn care can involve a mower, a gas can for the mower, a fertilizer spreader, bags of lawn food, and more. Keeping all this equipment in line makes the labor-intensive chore of yard care easier and more enjoyable. When organizing this zone, it's important to remember that everything must have a place of its own, and that different supplies and equipment in the zone should be grouped according to purpose.

YARD-CARE POWER TOOLS Gas or electric yard tools need to be stored properly to remain in good working order, away from traffic flow, and out of the reach of children.

- If you have a lawn mower with a folding handle, always fold it up and position it as out of the way as possible.

- Lawn mower accessories, such as a grass-catcher bag, should be cleaned out after every use and hung up, to keep the mess out of your storage area.

- Lightweight tools, such as weed trimmers, edgers, and hedge trimmers, should be hung up as well.

- Keep fuel for gas-powered tools locked up in a metal cabinet to prevent accidents.

- Seasonal equipment, such as snow blowers, should be stored in a corner. Always empty the fluids from seasonal equipment for off-season storage.

A backyard shed serves as handy overflow storage for frequently used garden tools, outdoor furniture cushions, and the like. This prefabricated unit can be assembled in less than an hour.

LONG-HANDLED TOOLS Rakes, shovels, hoes, and other long-handled yard tools should never just be left leaning against a wall or lying on a floor, where they create safety hazards.

- If you have the floor space, use a standing tool rack with separate cavities for each long-handled tool.

- More commonly, you'll find hanging racks with clip-in or slide-in handle holders, which will accommodate all kinds of tools, from spades with short, stocky handles to rakes with longer, thinner handles. Pick from simple hanging racks that support a few tools, or go for more complete structures with shelves, bins, and hose reels. No matter which type you buy, make sure it has the capacity to hold all your large, long-handled tools.

ABOVE LEFT Keep your garden tools together in a rack designed for them. This wall-mounted unit is sturdy and easy to install. ABOVE RIGHT A standing organizer has slots for a variety of long-handled garden implements. The unit itself is durable and easily cleaned, and can be moved out of the garage right to where the work will be done.

SMALL GARDENING TOOLS Hanging is a great way to store these, and many garden implements come with handle straps, holes, or rings so that they can be hung from pegs or hooks placed in a row. Even if the tools don't have straps, you can hang them with Peg-Board hooks on a small portion of Peg-Board. High-end garden-tool sets often come with their own durable storage cases, which let you keep all the tools together.

SUPPLIES The many supplies you use in landscaping your yard or maintaining your garden range in size and shape from small loose objects to oversize, hard-to-handle bags. Consequently, you need

an array of storage solutions. Keep all your garden supplies together on a sturdy shelving unit.

Bagged supplies, such as manure and lawn feed (and salt for the winter), can be stacked. But if your bags are prone to leakage, consider storing them in plastic tubs. Tubs are also a good idea for opened bags. If you don't use tubs, fasten with strong plastic clips to keep opened bags from leaking.

The best way to keep any outdoor supplies in order is to dedicate a set of shelves to them. Here, a cleanable plastic shelving unit is used for a full complement of gardening supplies.

Pot O' Tools: Create storage for small garden hand tools with the help of a terra-cotta or large plastic planter. Choose the size of pot that will accommodate all your hand tools, and stencil the word "tools" on the pot. Then place it on a shelf where you can get to the tools easily.

Round and Round: Garden hoses are a special storage challenge. Fortunately, there are many organizers available to keep your garden hose under control. Long hoses that must reach far corners of the yard can be wound onto hose caddies on wheels that offer maximum mobility. A hose bowl—a deep, decorative bowl that holds the wound-up hose—is a more basic and attractive solution. Metal hose reels are available in wall-mounted or stationary styles, and are also easy to use.

A durable foldup garden shed nests in the corner of a deck. This one has hangers and shelves to keep garden supplies and equipment in order.

Loose supplies, such as flower-bed markers, fertilizer spikes, and seed packets, are best kept in plastic boxes or trays on a shelf. Use a big enough container to ensure that the supplies are not jammed together. The containers should be labeled. Another option is to hang an organizer comprising canvas pockets (such as one used to organize shoes on the back of a door) on a wall stud or from the side of garage shelves. Group supplies by type in the different pockets.

Pots and planters should be stacked neatly and kept close to potting supplies. Keep plastic planters out of direct sunlight because too much exposure to direct sun can crack and fade unplanted plastic pots and boxes.

THE INSIDE SCOOP

Hammer Time: Nice as they look, you don't necessarily need a special hanging organizer for your long-handled tools. If you're willing to go with a slightly cruder solution, hammer large penny nails into a wall or stud, leaving enough room for the tool handle between the nails. Hang the tool upside down between the nails so that it is supported by its head.

Crafty Caddy: Bucket caddies are a wonderful way to keep your garden tools in order in a portable multipurpose organizer. The caddy is made of a tool belt wrapped around and attached to a 5-gallon plastic bucket. Take the tools and bucket wherever you go in your garden, and you'll have a place to put fresh-cut flowers, a handy hauler to move dirt from one place to the next, or a perfect place to toss weeds as you pull them out of the ground.

Devote a portion of the garage or shed to all your sports equipment. Everyone will always know where to find the gear—and where to put it back. Although you could cobble together a storage area with baskets, shelves, and cabinets, it's much wiser to buy custom racks

A sporting goods rack can keep all of your sports gear organized and ready to use—no matter their shapes and sizes. This durable rubber-and-plastic unit is sized just right to fit against the wall in a garage.

meant for storing exactly the equipment you have. Sporting goods manufacturers make storage devices for just about every type of equipment.

SKIS AND/OR SNOWBOARD RACKS You can buy individual hangers that keep snowboards or skis in place, but it usually makes more sense to purchase units integrated with shelving and hooks for boots, poles, and other accecssories.

BIKE-STORAGE SYSTEM The most basic types are coated wall hooks that support the frame of the bike. More advanced systems include bike trees that can store the bike horizontally or vertically, depending on available space. If you have lots of overhead clearance, consider a bike pulley system, where the bike is mounted on suspended supports and then hoisted overhead and out of the way.

FISHING GEAR RACKS These wire structures provide slots for several poles and plenty of space for a tackle box and a hanger for a net.

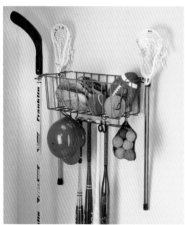 

Wall-mounted sports rack keeps sporting equipment up off the floor and collected where it's easy to reach. You can find specialized racks for just about any sporting goods.

MULTISPORT ORGANIZERS These are great choices if your family tends to play many different ball sports, such as baseball, tennis, and basketball, or if you have a lot of small accessories to store, such as knee pads and helmets for skateboarding. The organizer usually combines a large bin for loose balls and other items; hanging slots and hooks for bats and racquets; a shelf or small hangers for gloves, caps, and helmets; and additional storage accessories such as bins for smaller items.

Bikes can be in the way no matter where you put them, but mount them on the wall and they take up very little space.

ZONE 6

Car Care ⏱ 30 MINUTES

These days, most repairs relate to computerized functions within the car and are best left to professionals. But anyone who is willing to get his or her hands dirty can still save a little money by changing the oil, rotating the tires, and performing other basic car maintenance. And most people like to keep their cars clean. The best way

A well-organized garage leaves plenty of space for parking your car.

to keep car supplies organized is with a sturdy set of shelves. Wire "restaurant shelving" can be most effective, but other shelf units can work as well, as long as they are easily cleaned and have room for all your car supplies. To keep things simple, segregate supplies by function—keep extra oil and filters in one area, put all cleaning supplies on their own shelf, and so forth. Be sure to lock up these supplies to keep them away from curious children.

Maintaining Clutter-Free Garages and Sheds

Give your shed or garage a thorough cleaning twice a year—once in the spring before your planting and lawn mowing begin, and once in the fall as yard chores wind down. During these cleanings, remove everything from the space, sweep and clean it thoroughly, and then replace all your equipment and supplies. This will give you a chance to alter your organization as necessary, to check if any tools and equipment are damaged, and to find out if any bags or buckets of materials are leaking. Along with this biannual review, be sure to do the following:

1 Bin review

Do a weekly visual tour of the garage, making sure that your recycling bins are not overflowing. If they are, replace them with larger, or more, containers.

2 The maintenance moment

To keep your tools in good working order, regularly sharpen blades, clean moving parts, and lubricate mechanical pieces. Whenever you do this, make sure that your tools and equipment are stored where they won't be exposed to any kind of unusual wear.

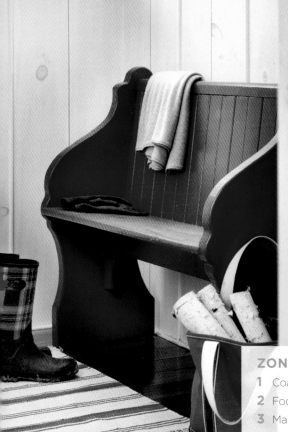

Foyers, Mudrooms, and Entryways

Entryways small and large are transitional areas where family members and visitors make the leap from outdoors to indoors, often bringing coats and sweaters, packages, and other clutter in with them. Keeping entry areas clutter-free means designing them for easy transitions. This should include elements that make it simple for everyone to see what should be left in the entryway (and where), and what should be brought into the house.

Your approach to clutter-proofing an entry room will vary depending on whether it is an informal entryway—the traditional "mudroom"—or a more formal foyer that is used by both family members and visitors. In many homes, these represent the rear-entry door and front door, respectively. The times assigned to each zone are based on an average-size space. If you have lots of children and visitors, leave a little extra time to organize the zones.

Entryways are not general, long-term storage spaces, and should not be used to store files or papers, extra serving plates, or sports equipment. Entryways are only for those things that come off when you enter the house and go on when you leave.

OPPOSITE A well-ordered entryway has a place for anything that might be brought into the home.

A single piece of furniture can help organize a small entryway, adding style as it brings order. This pretty hall bench "tree" is a perfect example of function and form.

1

A top shelf serves as a handy place for packages, laptop cases, and other items you want to remember to take with you on your way out the door.

2

A row of hooks provides accessible hanging storage for coats, scarves, handbags, and more. With the addition of a hanger, these can even be used for formal coats.

3

Compartments under the bench can be left open to store footwear or, as shown here, to fill with wicker baskets that hold boots on one side, and mittens, gloves, and caps on the other.

Coat Storage ⏱ 15 MINUTES

Coats and jackets need to have a specific place to hang in the entryway so they don't clutter other rooms in the house. The two basic types of coats that need to be hung and organized are informal jackets that can be placed on hooks, and more upscale cold-weather garments that should be hung on hangers. When planning the coat storage you need, be sure to take into account the room you'll need for your family's outerwear and for visitors' coats. If you have the space, seasonal outerwear can be hung in the entryway. If the closet is too cramped, you'll need to store cold-weather garments during the spring and summer in the attic, or wherever you have extra closet space.

COAT CLOSETS The entryway closet should be dedicated to coats.

- Often, the closet will include a shelf. This should be used for other outerwear items, such as mittens and hats, as necessary.

- Equip entryway closets with a collection of sturdy hangers—wood or heavy-duty plastic are best; don't use metal hangers that will bend under the weight of clothes.

- You can supply additional coat and sweater storage by attaching a rack with pegs or hooks to the back of the closet door.

- If small children are regulars in your entryway, mount a lower hanging bar in the closet. You can buy a short hanging bar to suspend from the regular closet rod by hooks and chains.

- Wherever you store the coats, try to create a section for each person so that everyone in the house can quickly find his or her jacket and accessories when heading out the door.

THE INSIDE SCOOP

Face Time: Children often pose a challenge in keeping the entryway clutter-free. To help young ones consistently put their coats and other outerwear in the right spot, put a picture of each child over the hook, cubby, or shoe area he or she is supposed to use.

FREESTANDING OPTIONS Many entryways don't have a closet, and even when they do, a freestanding piece of furniture can provide additional coat storage. If you have even a little extra space in your foyer, entryway, or mudroom, consider getting one.

Coatracks are the simplest storage solution for entryways.

- Tall and thin, they fit well in confined spaces.

- Racks can hold several jackets and caps, although they can be unstable when burdened with too many heavy coats.

- The big advantage to a coatrack is its portability; it can be positioned in the handiest location, out of direct traffic flow.

A freestanding coatrack is an efficient way to accommodate coats, hats, scarves, and other garments. This version makes the most of limited space by including an umbrella stand as part of the base.

One wall-mounted shelving unit can serve many purposes in the entryway. This one has ample shelf space on top, several compartments that can be assigned to different members of the family, and sturdy hooks for hanging garments.

- Some come equipped with umbrella stands integrated into the base construction.
- Choose between metal or wood, depending on which suits your entryway design best.
- If you have children, look for versions with midlevel hanging hooks in addition to the top "branches."

Hall trees are more complete storage solutions and better for busy households with many adults, children, and regular visitors. A hall tree is a single structure that includes a bench seat connected to a backboard, usually topped by a shelf, onto which hooks are fastened.

- Certain versions are made with a hanging rod that lets you suspend coats on hangers.
- Some come equipped with underbench shelves or cubbies, providing space off the floor for boots and shoes.
- Hall-tree benches are usually storage units themselves; the seat lifts up to reveal a chest space. This can be a handy location for scarves, mittens, umbrellas, and other inclement-weather gear.

Hooks and pegs give you the option of positioning hanging coat storage at eye level for the people in your household.

- Pegs are available in sets attached to a mounting base; buy individual hooks or hook sets, as needed.
- Quick to install and inexpensive, these are especially handy for small children.
- Be sure to buy hooks meant for coats (they are longer and thicker).
- If this will be the primary way you store coats and jackets, be sure to install enough for family members and for visitors.

Footwear 🕐 15 MINUTES

Ironically, shoes are second only to toys as annoying underfoot clutter. The process of keeping shoes organized begins with providing enough space for all the footwear in your entryway.

- Shoes need to be kept either on a mat or on a movable supporting rack so that the floor underneath can be cleaned regularly.

- In a formal foyer, you can use mats placed inside the closet under the coats.

- In a less formal entryway or where there's no closet, use attractive wooden or metal shoe racks to hold shoes and boots, or use a decorative wicker basket as an entryway accent and shoe organizer.

Keeping boots, shoes, and other footwear in order goes a long way toward keeping your entryway clutter-free. Stackable organizers are easy to clean and dividers keep each pair of shoes or boots in its own area.

THE INSIDE SCOOP

Sock Hop: Increasingly, American households are removing shoes in the entryway before entering the house proper—and there is a good reason to go shoeless in the home. The soles of most shoes track in dirt and allergens such as pollen. These pollutants can then get ground into rugs as people walk around the home, creating an unhealthy environment. To keep your home as pollutant-free as possible, provide an entryway rack or space where family members and visitors can put their shoes.

- Stackable shoe shelves are inexpensive and provide plenty of air circulation that will help wet shoes and boots to dry.

- No matter what you use to store shoes, it should be cleanable and able to catch dirt, salt, water, and so on.

- Keep shoes and boots in groups according to the person who wears them.

- If there is room, store boots in the entryway or foyer. If not, keep them in the bedroom closet during the off-season.

- Part of organizing the entryway should be removing the footwear that belongs somewhere else—basically any shoes or boots not specifically meant for inclement weather.

Mail and Keys 15 MINUTES

Although you usually deal with both keys and mail in the entryway, keys seem to disappear when you need them, while bills seem to accumulate when you don't. Both problems can be addressed with similar solutions—a specific place for them in the entryway.

KEYS Keep your keys from getting lost by giving them a specific place where they go the minute you walk in the door.

- You can use any of a number of key hangers available in a diversity of styles.

- You can also go the less expensive route of just mounting a hook for the keys on a wall or other nearby surface.
- If you have multiple sets of keys, keep them all in the same place.
- If you're reluctant to put anything more on the walls, keep keys in a decorative bowl or similar shallow container on a table or shelf by the door.

MAIL Take a little time to set up a mail station in the entryway.

- If you have open wall space, mount wood or metal wall files like those used for magazines, or hang a decorative fabric pouch.
- If you have a table in your entryway, use trays or bins to keep mail tidy.
- Whatever storage solution you use, keep it out in the open so that you'll see when you have a backlog of mail—and you'll be more likely to deal with it.

ZONE 4
Seasonal Storage 30 MINUTES

Seasonal items are all those things that get used specifically for different times of the year. These include umbrellas, mittens and gloves, hats and scarves, and gardening clogs and knee pads. For busy households and large families, a multibin organizer can keep the entryway in order. Each member of the family gets a bin for his or her own caps, hats, mittens, and other foul-weather gear.

UMBRELLAS Umbrellas should be stored standing up. When laid on their sides, the ribs can get damaged. The best umbrella stands allow for air circulation around the umbrellas so that they can dry. This doesn't mean you have to buy an umbrella stand; wicker or wire-mesh trash baskets can function perfectly well as umbrella holders.

SCARVES, MITTENS, AND GLOVES Scarves are generally hung up to make them accessible and to air them out. But they can be folded or rolled and stored in bins or baskets in the closet or on shelves or in cubbies in the entryway. Mittens and gloves need to be kept with their mates, and should be placed in storage that allows for air to circulate around them. A shallow woven or mesh tray or basket is ideal. If many people are using the entryway, consider including several clothespins for your mitten and glove storage, so that mates can be pinned together.

GARDENING GEAR If you are an avid gardener and like to put your garden togs on as you go out the door, the mudroom is a logical place to keep your favorite gardening shirt, clogs, knee pads, and apron. Garden footwear should be kept on a simple shoe rack that is easy to clean. Other gardening apparel can be kept in a bin or attractive basket on a shelf or on the floor by the back door.

A variety of hanging storage ensures this entryway can accommodate many visitors and coats short and long.

Maintaining Clutter-Free Foyers, Mudrooms, and Entryways

With enough hooks and other storage, entryways should stay orderly on their own because nobody spends much time there, but you still need to check the area periodically to keep it free of clutter.

1 Coat check

Every week, make sure coats are hung in their proper places. Rehang those that have fallen off their hooks or hangers, and put coats that have migrated to someone else's section of the closet back where they belong. When seasons change, make sure that you move heavy jackets and boots to seasonal storage spaces.

2 Disorderly conduct

Every 2 or 3 days, check on the orderliness of shoes and boots in the closet. Rearrange them, if necessary, so that they are easily accessible when needed.

3 Mail call

If you've equipped the foyer or entryway with a mail receptacle, do a Saturday-morning check to see that nothing important has been left in the receptacle, and that mail is being moved to where it needs to go.

ZONES

1 Desk
2 Technology and Equipment
3 Supplies and Reference Storage
4 Files

These days, the term "home office" covers many different work spaces, from well-equipped rooms used by people who telecommute or work at home full time, to compact corners or nooks where people pay bills, review paperwork, and conduct the business of keeping a household. If you're lucky, you have a whole room to dedicate to your home office. More likely, you'll have to make do with a smaller space.

That's not to say you have to work in messy quarters or deal with constant clutter. A small home office can function every bit as well as one that takes up a large room, as long as it is thoughtfully designed.

The organizational challenge of a home office is twofold: keeping household clutter from invading the work space, and preventing work items from cluttering other areas in the house. In both cases, loose papers are your enemy. That's why the first rule of home offices is to organize papers—in a file cabinet or on some sort of display organizer, like a bulletin board—or toss them.

If you have a bulletin board, keep it organized. Avoid bulletin-board clutter by not overlapping papers you hang up, by promptly taking down notices and other materials that are out of date, and by removing papers that should be filed. Group similar papers together on the bulletin board to make them easier to find, and always hang important papers at eye level to make them easy to read at a glance.

OPPOSITE Nestled in the corner of a room, this work space is a fully functional office with lots of storage.

A well-appointed office makes good use of small organizers that work with a wealth of concealed storage space.

1

Magazine cases are a great way to keep magazines, catalogs, manuals, and other reference materials organized and easy to find.

2

Wide "lateral" filing cabinets are built into the underdesk area, optimizing available space. No extra stand-alone cabinets are needed.

3

A quartet of wire in-trays keeps paperwork in order and holds a supply of fresh paper for printing and note-taking.

4

A mix of drawers and cabinets ensures that work items of all sizes have a place to go.

Of course, keeping papers in control is only part of the battle. You also want an office layout and accessories that make work easier, more efficient, and more comfortable, and where you can quickly find what you need. That's why your choices of a desk, reference storage, file organization, and technology are crucial. (If you rely heavily on a great deal of computer equipment in your office, assume that Zone 2, "Technology and Equipment," will take you extra time.) Choose wisely, and you'll end up with a tidy and attractive work area that promotes productivity.

STORAGE IN STYLE

Air Play: When desk space is at a premium, look for solutions out of thin air—hang bins and trays over the desk. Shop for organizing systems that clip onto the back edge or side of the desk and suspend trays, pen cups, and other accessories over the desk surface, leaving you plenty of space for your paperwork and files underneath. Be sure to leave room for your work space.

DOLLAR SMART

Office Door: Why pay a king's ransom for a large, stylish desk when you can make your own customized version for a lot less? Buy a hollow-core door, paint it your favorite color, and set it on two sawhorses painted a contrasting color for a stunning office focal point. Or lay the door across two half-height file cabinets to efficiently incorporate function with form.

Desk ⏱ 15 MINUTES

The important role the desk plays makes choosing the right one essential to beating clutter. First and foremost, your desk must be the right size for your needs. A desk that is too small makes it hard to work efficiently and keep the basic office tools at hand. But a desk that is too large becomes a wide, empty space that invites clutter.

DESKTOP Your desktop should provide enough room for basic office tools and have space to let you comfortably write, open your mail, and review files as necessary. There should be enough room around everything to allow for movement—so you don't bump your

computer monitor while reaching for a pencil. In figuring out how big your desk needs to be, you should work with the other zones of the home office. For example, you may prefer to use a desktop wire file-organizer for often-needed papers. But if the home-office space will not accommodate a large desk, those files are better placed in the front of your file cabinet or in a drawer.

Sometimes a home office will be used only as a place to pay bills and answer e-mail. This alcove off a kitchen supplies all the room necessary for an occasional work space.

THE INSIDE SCOOP

Shine On: Look to save desktop space with the home-office lighting you choose. Select adjustable desktop lamps with bases that are heavy enough to prevent tipping and thin bodies and necks that can focus the light exactly where you need it—and be swung out of the way when necessary. If you prefer a fixed lamp, make sure the body is narrow and the bulb and lamp shade are as small as possible while still providing the illumination you need.

In most home offices, the computer monitor, keyboard, and mouse form the central grouping of the desk, with other essentials positioned around this group. When setting up or reorganizing your desk, focus on the essentials.

Basic desktop implements such as pen and pencil holders, stapler, and tape dispenser should be grouped together. The best way to do this is to use an all-in-one organizer. These are available as stepped racks or as carousels. You can buy complete plastic or wood organizers with matching stapler, scissors, pencil sharpener, ruler, letter opener, staple remover, and tape dispenser.

In- and out-boxes are timeless organizing tools that no desk should be without. These can be wire, steel, plastic, or wood trays that are part of coordinated desk sets. You can also be creative and use decorative lacquered trays or other flat, shallow containers to suit your own tastes.

A mail organizer is also essential because the home office is the natural location for dealing with bills, direct-mail offers, catalogs, and other mail. Select from any number of slotted mail organizers to keep incoming and outgoing mail in order. Many of these can organize mail by date or subject, and some come with drawers underneath for envelopes, stamps, and other mail-related supplies.

ABOVE LEFT Where space or expense is an issue, you may not want to install cabinets or shelves. In that case, opt for desktop organizers such as these stackable units with compartments that keep supplies neat and accessible.
ABOVE RIGHT A month's worth of slots and two drawers make this mail organizer an excellent tool for keeping bills and other mail under control. Any good mail organizer should let you see individual envelopes, rather than stacks of them.

DRAWERS AND UNDERDESK STORAGE The problem with drawers is that everything is hidden. It's easy to put things there without thinking, and the drawers can quickly turn into clutter buckets. To make best use of your drawers and keep them as organized as possible, dedicate each drawer to one type of storage, and partition drawers, as necessary, to keep things neat. For example, use your top drawer to hold pens in a drawer organizer and to stack notebooks and paper for the printer. Even when the desk does not have drawers, the underdesk area can still be used for storage and organization. Keyboard trays attached to the underside of the desk give you a place to put your keyboard while keeping desk space free. When you are not using the computer, the keyboard slips underneath, out of sight. You can use the space where a row of drawers would normally be for rolling storage, such as a rolling file cabinet or a low, rolling printer stand.

Technology and Equipment

 30 MINUTES

Today's home office is usually equipped with some measure of technology, even if it's just an old computer and hand-me-down printer. The cords, peripherals, and odds and ends that go along with even a modest home-office setup are a big organizational challenge. The good news is that technological advances, such as wireless connectivity, can help you beat clutter.

COMPUTERS Making space for your computer is often the first step in setting up a home office. If you use a laptop, the space you'll need is modest—just a square foot or so of desktop space. If you have a more traditional desktop system, with a separate monitor, computer, keyboard, and mouse, you'll need more room.

- A computer tower can be placed on top of the desk, but taller ones tend to look awkward there and are often best stored under the desk. Make it easier to move the computer for cleaning or dealing with cords by mounting it on a stand or a wheeled trolley. Or buy computer hangers that mount to the underside of the desk and hold the unit up off the floor.

- Desktop computers can often support a small monitor placed on top. If you think the monitor is too heavy, buy a monitor stand big enough to allow the computer to slide underneath.

The monitor can be a big space hog on your desk, but it doesn't have to be. If it's time to update your equipment, consider buying a space-saving flat-panel monitor. If you have a traditional monitor, make the most of desk space by placing it on a monitor stand so that the space underneath it is still usable.

CORDS The various cords needed to connect different devices to each other and to a power source too often create an unsightly, dirt-collecting, disorderly mess. There are two basic options for keeping this particular clutter culprit in check: Keep all cords together, or do without them entirely. These strategies apply to all types of cords that transfer data to and between equipment, including cable and USB cords.

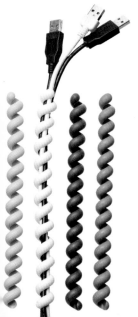

A cord organizer can be used to conceal your cords. There are two types: flexible tubes that keep the cords concealed so you can run a bundle of cords wherever they need to go, and rigid cord "channels" that also contain all your cords in one outer shell. Although less flexible, the channels are more easily attached to surfaces such as the underside of your desk or wall baseboards. Lengths of rigid channels are put together by combining sections of straight pieces and corner "elbows." Both flexible and rigid organizers are available in a wide selection of colors, finishes, and materials. You can also choose from simple, less-expensive plastic braces with clip-in slots for cables and wires. One is positioned about every foot to keep the cords and wires untangled and running parallel for their length.

Go wireless for a streamlined, more complete solution. Many of today's computers, peripherals, and input devices (keyboards and mice) offer wireless models and solutions. For building wireless home networks, Wi-Fi is the protocol. This technology lets you surf the Web, share files between computers, and even print—all without wires. For mice, keyboards, and printers, infrared or Bluetooth technology can be used to eliminate the wires between peripherals and the PC.

DIGITAL CAMERAS AND MUSIC PLAYERS Today's computers let you download music and upload images from digital cameras to your computer and have special ports for cables that connect the music player or camera to the computer. When you are not downloading or uploading, store the camera and music player in an appropriate area away from the home office so that they don't clutter the desktop and risk getting broken. A digital camera can be stored in a box or in its own case along with your other photographic equipment or photos. If you tend to use the music player when you go out, keep it where you store your wallet and other everyday items. Otherwise, store it in a drawer or other safe place.

PRINTER Although high-quality printers have gotten smaller over time, they still take up a great deal of surface area. You also need room to remove or insert paper and replace ink cartridges, further complicating printer placement.

- You can make efficient use of desktop space by placing a printer on a desktop printer stand. Available in clear acrylic, colored plastic, metal, or wood, printer stands range from simple platforms that create an empty storage space underneath to more complex workstations with multiple drawers, cord channels, shelves, and other features.

- If your home office has the floor space, you can place the printer on an independent printer stand with room for reams of paper, supplies, and more.

- You can even buy a mobile workstation with room for other devices, such as a fax and a scanner. Just be aware that cords will limit how mobile the station can be.

THE INSIDE SCOOP

Screening Room: Desktop cramped for space? Make use of the sides of your computer monitor with a monitor-top organizer. Made in different sizes, these organizers fit across the top of the monitor and have pockets hanging on each side. The pockets can be used to hold small items such as pens, stamps, and so on. These organizers don't work on flat-screen monitors.

Tied Up: Turn to your local home center or hardware store for an inexpensive and effective cord organization solution. Industrial connector ties—professional versions of the twist ties you use for garbage bags—are easy to use and can keep a group of cables or wires bundled securely together.

SCANNER Today's home computer stations often include a scanner that lets you scan older photos or art for party invitations, holiday greeting cards, and more. Where you place your scanner depends on how often you use it, how much desk space you have, and the length of its cables.

- If you tend to use it only once a month, you might want to keep the scanner on a shelf, moving it to the desk when you use it.

- If you use it more often, find space for the scanner on your desk, or use a desktop printer stand so that you still have room beneath the scanner.

- Consider purchasing a combination scanner/printer/fax machine to save space.

TELEPHONE AND FAX Phones don't have to take up a lot of room in the home office. Most phones come with brackets that allow them to be mounted on the wall. You may prefer to use a cordless phone and keep the base station in another room, closer to an installed phone jack. If you use a headset when working in your home office, be sure that it has a place to go when you're not using it, such as a hook or a desktop cradle. If you only use a cell phone in your home office, keep a spare charger nearby.

THE INSIDE SCOOP

Paperless Possibilities: Your computer isn't just an organizational lifesaver in the home office; it can also be a clutter solution. Inexpensive software packages let you manage lists of contacts, day-to-day calendars, checking and savings accounts, and more. Use your computer to capacity and you can toss your address book, calendar, and a host of other paper files. If you feel uncertain about going paperless, then back up your data on a regular basis and keep hard copies of all your important items.

A dedicated printer stand keeps all printed documents and printer supplies in order. A convenient wheeled unit allows you to move the printer out of the way when not in use.

THE INSIDE SCOOP

Printer Hideaway: If you have a large desk with lots of room underneath, consider a rolling printer stand. It is short enough to fit right under the desk, and usually comes with an additional shelf for paper or other supplies. When you need to print a document, just pull the printer out from under the desk.

Running Interference: Be aware that wireless devices and home networks can be disrupted by the signals of cordless phones operating at certain frequencies (microwave ovens may also cause disruption). If you are experiencing problems with wireless accessories, temporarily replace your cordless phone with a traditional unit to test whether the phone is the problem.

Traditional fax machines present the same organizational challenges that printers do. Not only do you need to make room for the fax machine itself, you also need room for a paper supply and output. In addition, the fax machine will need to be connected to a phone line that has to be run from the nearest phone jack. That's why the best option is often a computer "onboard" fax system. You can buy computer software that will let you fax documents directly from your computer to an outside number, through your Internet service. The drawback of this technique is that you can't fax existing paper documents, but if you have a scanner, you can scan documents into the computer and then fax them.

COPIERS AND MULTIPURPOSE UNITS If you regularly use a copier in your home office, or have a multipurpose machine (one that includes a variety of functions, such as copying, faxing, and scanning), set up a dedicated station for it. The unit can sit atop a stationary cabinet or a cart with wheels, but the support structure should have enough room underneath for extra paper, replacement ink and cartridges, scanner bulbs, and other replacement supplies. The top surface of the cart or cabinet should have room for the copier or combination unit and a tray to hold copies that need to be made, faxes that have just come in, and other documents.

ZONE 3
Supplies and Reference Storage

 I HOUR

Whether you're using a home office for writing a novel, running a real estate business, or just trying to keep bills straight and the household running, you'll need space for supplies and reference materials. In most home offices, shelves are the best option for storing these items. Open storage lets you see what you have and what you need, and find books, magazines, and manuals without having to search high and low. You can choose between stand-alone shelf units and wall-mounted shelves. Make your decision based on how much shelf space you need, your available office space, and what you need to store. For example, if you need to store only a few magazines and some office supplies, a wall-mounted shelf may offer all the space and stability necessary. But if you have more floor space and need to store multiple reams of paper and thick reference books, you'll probably want to use a self-standing bookshelf.

Flame Free: Every home office can benefit from a fireproof safe. Use the safe for extremely important documents, such as birth certificates and essential letters that exist only in paper form. Find affordable fireproof safes at home centers, hardware stores, office supply stores, and large discount retailers. Put the safe in an inconspicuous location, but one that you can easily access when necessary.

Paper and stationery supplies are best kept neatly stacked on shelves. Keep them away from any water sources, such as a fish tank or water cooler, and heat sources, such as a radiator or space heater. Store reams of papers upright on their edges, by type (for example, regular paper, photo-grade paper, and three-hole-punched paper). If you don't have a bookend or other firm support on the shelf next to the paper, keep the different papers in file folders.

Magazines are best kept organized in magazine racks. These standing boxes have cutouts that let you see the spines of the magazines and easily grab any individual issue.

Books should be grouped by type so you can easily and quickly find the reference you need at any given time. Heavier books, such as large dictionaries, should be kept on lower shelves to prevent standing shelves from tipping and attached shelves from pulling away from the wall. Use bookends rather than books stacked on their sides at the end of a row; stacked books are more difficult to pull out.

Office supplies come in all sizes and shapes, from individual pens to boxes of staples to loose rolls of tape. To accommodate the variety, keep office supplies in a dedicated box or bin on the shelf, or in drawers by type of supply.

OPPOSITE **Make the best use of office shelves by placing labeled boxes to hold supplies, files, and reference materials on them. This office also has a ready-made organizer unit with space for a printer, hanging files, and slide-out bins in a range of sizes.**

One of the biggest challenges in keeping your home office in order is your filing system. Start by reviewing all your paper files. Throw out what you no longer need and move files such as old tax returns to long-term storage in the attic or garage. Once you've pared down your files to what you absolutely need to store, plan your filing system. Take a few minutes to map out the titles of the hanging file folders in your cabinet, and the files within those hanging folders. Once you have planned the order of your files, reorganize them within the file cabinet. Of course, the cabinet you use will depend on the space in your home office and the way you prefer to work. File cabinets come in diverse shapes and sizes, from half-height, two-drawer units to tall, wide lateral-file cabinets. You'll find file cabinets and cases in wood, metal, plastic, and more unusual combinations, such as fabric or wicker around a steel-wire frame.

ROLLING FILES Rolling file cabinets let you easily move the files around in the space as your needs change.

- Rolling cabinets are limited to two-drawer, half-height models; taller four-drawer units would be prone to tipping over if placed on casters.

- The simplest version of a mobile filing unit is the trolley, an open frame with wheels. The files hang from fixed runners along the top of the frame. Some have two levels, but this feature only increases the natural instability of these types of units. Not only are they more likely to tip over than solid-sided cabinets, the framework lets file folders slip out of the sides of hanging folders. Consequently, if you choose a trolley-type cabinet, pick one with solid sides.

Shelving keeps reference materials in order in this streamlined, minimalist home work space.

STATIONARY CABINETS File cabinets that sit flat on the floor are the more traditional home office choice. The two types are lateral and vertical. Files in lateral cabinets hang so that they face the sides of the wide cabinets. Vertical file cabinets are more common in home offices—the files are arranged front to back in the cabinet. Stationary cabinets are usually more stable than wheeled units, especially when the cabinet is loaded with files; the weight transfer when a file drawer is opened or closed is more evenly distributed in a stationary cabinet than it would be with wheels.

A stationary cabinet with vertical files can help you banish stacks of paper forever.

THE FILE QUESTIONS

The best way to organize your files well is to answer three basic questions.

1. Do your files have a system? You should be able to concisely explain how your filing system works, and finding a file should be simple and intuitive. One of the best filing methods is a simple alphabetic system organized by the first letter of the topic. You also want to keep the file papers in order, so that any single file is organized from newest papers in front to the oldest in back, or vice versa.

2. Do you have enough space for your files? If you are cramming files into an overstuffed cabinet, you may be tempted to throw away essential papers, and you will have trouble accessing the ones you need. Perform a realistic assessment of your file-storage needs and add another cabinet if you need it.

3. Can you digitize some of your paper files? These days, much of what we formerly retained and stored as paper can be converted to computer files. Taxes and banking can be done online and stored on a disc, copies of correspondence can be kept on your hard drive, and product information is often available at companies' Web sites or as software supplied with electronic products. Digitizing paper files can make organizing them an easier task, and makes for less paper clutter. Make sure you keep a hard copy of vital records and documents, though.

Maintaining Clutter-Free Home Offices and Work Spaces

Home offices need to be regularly monitored to ensure that clutter is not getting in the way of productivity. Periodic spot-checks help you stay ahead of clutter and keep the office as organized as possible.

1 The telltale snapshot

Once each week, walk into your work space and take a mental snapshot of your desk. Are papers strewn about? Are computer discs loose in a messy pile? Put the desk back in order, paying special attention to any papers or items that don't have a logical place to go. Buy new organizational aids as needed to refine your workspace and accommodate the way you work, and take a few minutes to return everything to its rightful place so that you can work with a clear space—and a clear mind.

2 Shelf shuffle

Every 2 weeks, check your shelf inventory of supplies, and order paper, ink cartridges, and anything else you need.

3 Filed down

Every 6 months, go through your files to determine if any are no longer in use and should be archived. Check that files are not crammed into the file cabinet. If they are, buy another file cabinet. During this review, go through your files and make sure they are logically organized so that everything is easy to find.

CHAPTER 10
Laundry Rooms

ZONES

1 Supplies Storage
2 Ironing Station
3 Drying and
  Folding Area
4 Soaking Area

Your laundry room location is dictated by power and water lines and the venting necessary for a dryer to operate. This means that sometimes the laundry room may not be a room at all; it might be a corner of the basement or an alcove off the kitchen. It may even be located in the garage. But no matter where your laundry room is situated, the chosen area should provide clearance enough to maneuver around the washer and dryer, adequate storage for laundry supplies, and, ideally, a place to fold and iron clothes.

The organization challenge in a laundry room is to set it up so you can do everything in there efficiently. Everything in a laundry room should have a place to go when not in use. For example, if you leave your ironing board out at all times, it will become a parking place for a wide array of clutter. Without an established folding area, newly dried clothes tend to migrate all over the laundry room—and beyond. Fortunately, the laundry room has a clearly designed function. The only purposes you need to account for are washing, drying, folding, and ironing clothes.

OPPOSITE Storage is style in this chic laundry room, which brings together shelves, baskets, a tall laundry cart, and a hanging rod to create a highly efficient, workable space.

A neat laundry room combines different types of storage to serve a multitude of needs.

1
....
Cabinets with safety latches keep detergents and other hazardous materials away from children.

2
....
A rod positioned over the sink lets you hang ironed items.

3
....
Open shelving can be used for frequently needed items or for small loose supplies.

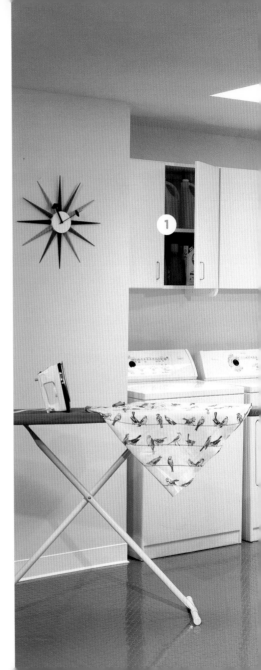

4

A deep sink lets you soak stained items, and provides a good place for garments to drip-dry.

5

A wall-mounted unit offers a stable surface for folding clothes, as well as bins to hold folded items. The pullout bins can be removed to carry clean clothing.

6

Undercounter baskets allow for easy laundry sorting,

243

Supplies Storage 30 MINUTES

Storage for laundry-room supplies need not be extensive because there is only so much you'll need to store. However, if you are looking to buy laundry supplies in bulk, consider a complete laundry-center unit. These bracket the washer and dryer with shelves and cabinets and can often supply the storage space you need for cleaning supplies, baskets to organize clothes for washing and folding, and more. In many cases, a more modest amount of storage will be sufficient. You can opt for cabinets or shelving—whichever suits the space and your preferences. Shelves are generally less expensive and easier to put up. Whichever type of storage you choose to use, the key is to position the storage above or close to the washer and dryer, where the supplies will be used.

LAUNDRY SUPPLIES Whether you use cabinets or shelves, keep supplies separated by type, using organizers for groups of smaller items. For example, keep stain and spot removers and stain pre-treatments in their own tray. To make things even easier, keep your supplies in order of use near where you use them, with detergent, bleach, and fabric softener organized in that order near the washing machine, and dryer sheets kept near the dryer. Consider washer and dryer pedestals with storage drawers. Your washer or dryer is placed on the pedestal, which not only gives you storage space

STORAGE IN STYLE

Magnetic Personality: Keep small supplies you use most often, like dryer sheets, stain remover, and other fairly light bottles or boxes, close at hand with a magnetic organizer hung on the side of your washing machine. These are available as simple net bags with magnetic hangers or sturdier plastic bins with stronger magnetic attachments.

in the drawer, but also raises the height of the unit, reducing your need to bend to do laundry. However, if there are children in your home, dangerous supplies such as bleach must go on shelves or cabinets well out of their reach, or in locked cabinets next to the washer or dryer.

A wire shelf unit stands over the washer and dryer and supports folded items. The foldout arm accommodates hanging clothes.

This organizer hangs on the back of a closet door, storing as many supplies as a large cabinet could.

LAUNDRY You won't always be able to wash dirty clothes the minute you bring them into the laundry room, so you'll need to make room near the washer for "incoming" loads. You may need more than one laundry basket if you have a large family or you want to presort. If you presort your clothes before washing, use hampers to make the process easier. Three simple canvas or mesh baskets on a shelf—for bright colors, darks, and whites— can help you organize dirty laundry for washing, keep the clothes off the floor, and make sure that dirty clothes never find their way into piles of clean laundry waiting to be folded. You can buy manufactured laundry-sorter units made up of three mesh or fabric bags in a single chrome or wood frame.

INSIDE SCOOP

Portable Places: In some situations, such as garages with cement walls, hanging cabinets or shelves will be very difficult, if not impossible, to install. That doesn't mean you have to do without effective storage. You can find independent laundry-room carts and shelf stands at bed and bath shops and home centers. Some are thin shelving units that fit neatly in the confined space between the washer or dryer and adjacent walls. For convenient storage, choose a trolley unit that can be wheeled where you need it and then out of the way when the laundry is done.

Ironing is generally not a favorite task, but if you use the right board and ironing-station organizer, the chore will be easier and more pleasant, and the board will never get in the way of the other things you have to do in the laundry room. Your choice of ironing board will basically come down to using a mounted board or a freestanding unit.

MOUNTED IRONING BOARDS A major advantage to wall-mounted boards is the access underneath. They let you iron difficult pieces, such as dresses and pants, more easily by permitting the clothes to slide further onto the board without being impeded by board legs. There are two types of mounted boards: recessed and surface-mounted. Recessed boards are completely hidden and out of the way when stored, while surface-mounted boards just fold up against the mounting platform in plain view.

Recessed (or hidden) ironing boards are a stylish option. The cabinet doors and interiors are available in many surface treatments such as oak or pine. The recessed cabinet can be built to include storage for the iron and ironing supplies. Recessed

A wall-mounted ironing board unit lets you flip the board up and out of the way when not in use, concealed in a handsome wood cabinet.

boards require substantial modification of an existing wall.

Surface-mounted ironing boards fold up and out of the way just as recessed boards do, but the surface-mounted version is more easily installed. The basic mounting plate and hinge unit can be attached to wall studs and masonry walls fairly simply. With this type of board, you'll need to create a separate place, or another nearby spot, for the iron and ironing supplies. A shelf above the board unit is often the best solution.

FREESTANDING IRONING BOARDS These are the simplest and least expensive ironing boards.

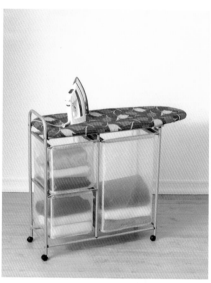

- Most boards are adjustable for different heights, and you can select from different lengths.

- You can store your freestanding board on a hanging organizer that includes hooks for the board and a bin or shelf for the iron and supplies. This organizer is attached to the wall or hung from the side of a tall shelving unit or cabinet.

- If you don't have any wall space for your board, you can buy a board hanger that mounts on the back of a door or hangs from the top of the door.

This combination ironing board and laundry cart makes the most of any space. The mesh bag compartments can be used for ironed folded items, or to separate laundry loads prior to washing. The board is detachable and the bags are removable.

Drying and Folding Area ⏱ 30 MINUTES

Folding clothes at a designated station in the laundry room is one way to diminish the possibility that clothes will become bedroom clutter. Unfolded clothes are too easily laid on a bed or chair to be folded later. It makes sense to include drying facilities in this zone because drying the clothes prepares them for folding or hanging.

DRYING AIDS There are many types of structures to efficiently dry clothes in the space you have available.

Drying racks come in all shapes and sizes, in wood, plastic, and metal. Many are expandable, and some include flat drying shelves as well as the traditional bars for drying. If you dry mostly loose items such as stockings, socks, and undergarments, a basic rack may do the trick. If you tend to dry delicate blouses or sweaters, you'll

ABOVE LEFT Retractable clotheslines can be used indoors or out, mounting quickly and easily to a wall. ABOVE RIGHT A foldout drying rack attaches to a wall or solid door, and collapses almost flat. Pulled out, the rack holds a small laundry load's worth of garments.

A simple stackable dryer can be handy for drying delicates and sweaters. It can be placed over a sink or on a countertop—even on top of your dryer.

probably need a rack with drying shelves. On metal drying racks, the bars should be coated or stainless steel to avoid staining delicate fabrics.

A drying line can be an excellent option in laundry rooms that are cramped for floor space, but with plenty of overhead space. You can use a regular clothesline running between hooks attached to two facing walls or a "hotel-style" retractable drying line.

Foldout hanging bars are attached to a wall or the back of a door for hang-drying loose garments or storing newly pressed shirts and clothes on hangers. These types of bars can be folded out of the way when not in use.

THE INSIDE SCOOP

Sink Smarts: A large laundry-room sink can do double duty as a table for folding clothes. Where space is at a premium, use a removable sink cover as a folding area. Find sink covers at home centers.

FOLDING SPACE Every laundry room benefits from a specific area for folding laundry. You don't need a lot of space because you can fold only one garment at a time.

- A deep countertop is best, because it lets you completely lay out whatever you are folding.

- If your laundry room does not have a countertop, customize one. Create a folding surface out of a piece of plywood or sheet of hard plastic large enough to fit over the top surface of your dryer, or washer and dryer. Fold the clothes on top as you pull them out of the dryer. Or use a hinged countertop crafted from a piece of plywood and sturdy hinges attached to the wall.

- Keep hangers near the ironing board. Hang shirts and other permanent-press items on them as soon as they come out of the dryer so that you won't have to iron them.

- Use a wall- or door-mounted folding hanging rod or a hanging stand to keep garments in order until you put them away.

THE INSIDE SCOOP

Pop and Dry: Sweaters can be difficult garments to dry, but "pop-open" sweater dryers work fast and easily. Pop open the sweater dryer (it looks like a potato chip made out of window screen) and lay the garment over the curve of the dryer. The shape of the dryer and its screened body allow for maximum air circulation and quick drying. When you're done, just fold the dryer up and store it on a shelf or in a cabinet.

Bag Time: Mesh bags are wonderful for washing lingerie and other delicates, but they need a place to go when not in use. Hang the bags from hooks on the wall or under a cabinet or shelf positioned over the washing machine. This will ensure that they are within arm's reach when you're sorting clothes to go into the washing machine, and hanging them will allow them to dry after use.

Soaking Area   🕐 15 MINUTES

Every laundry room should have a durable "slop sink" for soaking garments and hand-washing delicates, such as sweaters. Hang a rag or paper-towel dispenser within arm's reach of the sink so that you can clean up spills as soon as they occur. Keep a wire or plastic-mesh bin in the sink as a place to put garments to drain so you still have access to the sink.

Maintaining Clutter-Free Laundry Rooms

Because life is so busy, the laundry area can easily fall into disarray. Here's how to make sure your laundry area stays free of clutter.

1 ### Inventory analysis

Before your weekly grocery-shopping trip, check the supplies-storage area of your laundry room. Return supplies that have been scattered about the room to their proper area, and check for items that need to be replenished.

2 ### Orphan patrol

Once a week—not when you're doing laundry—visit the laundry room to check for leftover soaking, dried, or dirty clothes. Return these orphans to their correct locations.

Photography Credits

Michel Arnaud: 10

Courtesy California Closets: 38, 49, 61, 63, 97, 182, 187, 213, 218–219, 235, 236, 242–243

Gemma Comas: 44

Courtesy of The Container Store, www.containerstore.com: 19, 21 (left), 32, 84, 86, 95, 163 (bottom), 225 (bottom), 232, 240

Corbis: 120; Image Source, 43; Laura Johansen/Beateworks, 184; Elliott Kaufman/Beateworks, 4; Kate Kunz, 150; Ocean 57; Radius Images, 116, 145; Andrea Rugg/Beateworks, 160

Carlos Domenech: 126

Philip Esparza: 134

Getty Images: 139; Agence Images, 70; Peter Anderson, 215; Comstock, 170; Creative Crop, 106; Datacraft Co Ltd., 92; Vanessa Davies, 80; Charlie Drevstam, 54; Yvonne Duivenvoorden, 201; Gallo Images, 221; Glow Décor, 41, 42, 90; Image Source, 100; Rick Lew, 239; Charles Maraia, 9; Andrew McCaul, 34; Rob Melnychuk, 103; Steven Mark Needham/FoodPix, 143; Siede Preis, 166; Howard Rice, 181; Tetra Images, 62, 107; Matthew Ward, 198; Steve Wisbauer, 25

Courtesy of Gidden: 81

Tria Giovan: 136

Courtesy of Grange Furniture, Inc., www.grange.fr: 148–149, 158

Brian Hagiwara: 74

Bill Holt: 133

Courtesy of Home Depot: 191

IPC Syndication: Douglas Gibb, 104; Douglas Gibb/Ideal Home, 6; Bruce Hemming/Beautiful Kitchens, 22 (left); Simon Scarboro/Woman & Home, 125; Mark Scott/Ideal Home, 58; Tim Young/Ideal Home, 72

iStockphoto: Doug Cannell, 39; Norman Chan, 96; Digital Paws Inc, 226 (bottom); Ernesto Diaz, 50; Eddison Photos, 176; Joe Gough, 24; HSN-Photography, 230; Carlos Gawronski, 88; Alex Gul, 226 (top); Altay Kaya, 225 (top); Sarah Lee, 14, 20, 53, 142, 220; Logorilla, 178; Luso Images, 154;

Sherwin McGehee, 59; Miquel Munill, 228 (top); Werner Münzker, 29 (top); Keith Muratori, 129; Skip Odonnell, 222; Morten Olsen, 28; Paga Design, 132; Pearleye, 210; Polarica, 65; Resavskyi, 67; Pavlo Sachek, 174; Angelika Schwarz, 163 (top); Spauln, 37 (top); Emrah Turudu, 51; Vika Valter, 22 (right); Matka Wariatka, 36 (top); Nicole Waring, 64 (left); Ivonne Wierink-Van Wetten, 155; Camilla Wisbauer, 29 (middle)

Frances Janisch: 216

Courtesy of J.C. Penney: 76–77, 85, 109 (left), 122 (left), 199, 202, 204, 207, 229

Courtesy of KraftMaid Cabinetry, www.kraftmaid.com: 17 (right), 18 (right), 26

Courtesy of Lillian Vernon, www.lillianvernon.com: 23, 52, 60, 64 (right), 79, 82 (right), 87, 98, 112 (right), 115 (right), 118 (right), 121, 185, 211, 223 (right), 247, 248, 249, 250

Courtesy of Ligne Roset, www.ligne-roset-usa.com: 137

David Livingston: 110

Loupe Images: Ryland Peters & Small Ltd.: 30, 44, 146, 156, 159

Michael Luppino: 151

Jeff McNamara: 46–47

Peter Murdock: 130

Courtesy Plain & Fancy Custom Cabinetry, www.plainfancycabinetry.com: 15, 21 (right)

Courtesy of Rubbermaid, www.rubbermaid.com: 18 (left), 36 (bottom), 37 (bottom), 66, 68, 82, 99, 109 (right), 112 (left), 115 (left), 118 (left), 122 (right), 123, 165, 168, 173, 175, 177, 179, 189, 192 (right), 193, 194 (bottom), 196, 197, 209, 223 (left), 245, 246

Brad Simmons: 71

Beth Singer: 12–13

Courtesy of Stacks and Stacks, www.stacksandstacks.com: 206

Stockfood: Braun/GU, 16

Courtesy of Wood-Mode Fine Custom Cabinetry, www.wood-mode.com: 17 (left), 33, 25, 40

Cover: none; Spine: none; Back Cover: iStockphoto, Werner Münzker (left), Spx Chrome (center), Pearleye (right)

Index

Note: For references that include photographs, page numbers indicate the corresponding caption.

HEARST BOOKS

New York

An Imprint of Sterling Publishing
387 Park Avenue South
New York, NY 10016

Good Housekeeping is a registered trademark of Hearst Communications, Inc.
© 2005 by Hearst Communications, Inc.

All rights reserved. No part of this publication may be reproduced, stored in a retrieval system, or transmitted, in any form or by any means, electronic, mechanical, photocopying, recording, or otherwise, without prior written permission from the publisher.

Every effort has been made to ensure that all the information in this book is accurate. However, due to differing conditions, tools, and individual skills, the publisher cannot be responsible for any injuries, losses, and/or other damages that may result from the use of the information in this book.

ISBN 978-1-61837-041-9

Library of Congress Cataloging-in-Publication Data
Peterson, C. J.

Good housekeeping clutter rescue: organize your house for good / C. J. Peterson.

p. cm.

Rev. ed. of: The complete clutter solution. c2005.

Includes bibliographical references and index.

1. Home economics. 2. Housekeeping. I. Complete clutter solution. II. Title.

TX147.P39 2008

648—dc22

2008007950

Distributed in Canada by Sterling Publishing

c/o Canadian Manda Group, 165 Dufferin Street

Toronto, Ontario, Canada M6K 3H6

Distributed in the United Kingdom by GMC Distribution Services

Castle Place, 166 High Street, Lewes, East Sussex, England BN7 1XU

Distributed in Australia by Capricorn Link (Australia) Pty. Ltd.

P.O. Box 704, Windsor, NSW 2756, Australia

For information about custom editions, special sales, and premium and corporate purchases, please contact Sterling Special Sales at 800-805-5489 or specialsales@sterlingpublishing.com.

Manufactured in China

2 4 6 8 10 9 7 5 3 1

www.sterlingpublishing.com